Julie Sahni's

Introduction to
Indian Cooking

Julie Sahni's
Introduction to

Indian Cooking

Photography by Ben Fink

TEN SPEED PRESS
Berkeley, California

Ten Speed Press
P.O. Box 7123
Berkeley, California 94707

A Kirsty Melville book

Distributed in Canada by Publishers Group West, in New Zealand by Tandem Press, in South Africa by Real Books, in Southeast Asia by Berkeley Books, and in the United Kingdom and Europe by Airlift Books.

Cover and text design by Toni Tajima
Photography by Ben Fink

Library of Congress Cataloging-in-Publication Data

Julie Sahni's Introduction to Indian Cooking
p. cm.
Includes index.
ISBN 0-89815-976-8 (pbk.)
1. Cookery, Indic. I. Title.
TX724.5.I4S2414 1998
641.5954—dc21 97-35974
CIP

First printing, 1998
Printed in The United States of America

1 2 3 4 5 6 7 8 9 10 — 02 01 00 99 98

Contents

Acknowledgments

"Write a book of simple, delicious food you serve us (family and friends) that will introduce Indian cooking to a novice in a small town, such as Flint, Michigan," said my beloved friend, the late Pierre Franey. He sowed the seeds for this book, for which I am eternally indebted.

I also thank my mother, Padmavati Ranganathan, for helping me gather recipes, and passing along innovative suggestions, saying thing like, "Try Rice Krispies in the fritter batter for a great crunchy texture."

As the book concept became a reality, many colleagues extended generous help and valuable suggestions. In particular Susan Derecskey, who edited this book; Pat Adrian of Book of the Month Club for bringing Kirsty Melville, the publisher of Ten Speed Press and me together; Nach Waxman of Kitchen Arts and Letters; Bill Wallace of Draegers, and Daniel Halpern of the Ecco Press.

At Ten Speed Press, I thank my editor, Mariah Bear, for her devoted determination, for ensuring that every operation goes through her scrutinizing eyes, and laboring over details until we got it "just right." I am also thankful to Joan Nielsen for her painstakingly meticulous proofreading, and to Toni Tajima for an incredibly captivating book design.

Finally, a special thank you to photographer Ben Fink whose lucid still-life photos brilliantly capture my food. Thank you also to food and prop stylist Lauren Huber for her uncompromising eye to details; and Gerri Sarnataro Weiner, Director of Peter Kump's Cooking School, for her tireless work as prop and chef's assistant, staying focused even when hit by a violent virus during the shoot. It was indeed my privilege to have worked with such a talented and spirited photographic team as I prepared all the food for photographs at the Julie Sahni's School of Indian Cooking studio.

INTRODUCTION

WELCOME to the fascinating world of Indian cuisine! Based on the very principles so much in favor today—the preference for healthful wholesome foods and the passion for exciting new flavors—Indian cooking is perfectly suited to the Western kitchen and palate.

I would like to dispel the notion that Indian cooking is exotic, complex, and time-consuming. One reason for this misconception is the long list of ingredients, primarily spices, in Indian recipes. But they are there for a reason. While other cuisines use ingredients such as cornstarch, cream, and vinegar to thicken, enrich, and lend a sour taste, Indian cooking uses spices to do all these jobs, plus more. Spices have many properties besides the aromatic and medicinal. Indian cooks have capitalized on all the attributes of spices, and they are the underpinnings of Indian cooking. Mention spices and instantly visions of snake-charmers, gaily festooned elephants, and the Taj Mahal shimmering in the moonlight come to mind. Yet it may come as a surprise to find that only a handful of spices are native to India, black pepper, cardamom, turmeric, and kari leaf among them. Most of the spices in curry powder, the famous spice blend from India, are of Mediterranean origin. Cumin, coriander, fennel, mustard, and fenugreek are all native to the Mediterranean Basin. And chiles, too, are an import, introduced by the Portuguese in the early sixteenth century from the New World.

Indian cooking is not one single style of cooking. Rather, it is an amalgamation of several cuisines representing the different geographical features of the nation, its cultural heritage, and the religious beliefs of its people. The terrain and climate of India are indeed extremely varied. They range from snow-covered Kashmir in the northern Himalayan mountains to the sultry Malabar coast in the deep south, from the lush slopes of Darjeeling in the east to the sprawling Rajasthan desert of the west. India has also been gastronomically influenced by invading cultures over the centuries. These include everyone from the Greeks, Arabs, and Mongols to the Portuguese and British.

These shifts in climate, culture, and religious practices have spawned a bountiful array of foods from each region. From the north come mellow yogurt-and-herb marinated and grilled meats, the most famous being tandoori chicken; subtle curries of lamb and kid; smoky pan-roasted vegetables; garlicky lentils; and sweet, fruity yogurt drinks. Braised meat is scented with cumin, fennel, and cardamom and the spice blend called *garam masala*. Bread is the staple there, made with whole-grain flours from wheat, millet, and corn. North India is also the land of fragrant basmati rice. Food is cooked in amber colored oils pressed from mustard seeds or peanuts and is garnished with fresh coriander and mint.

In the south, the homeland of the Hindu Brahmin and Jain vegetarians, food is more earthy and fiery. Curried stews with lentils, steamed vegetables dressed with coconut and mustard seeds, and assertive tamarind-flavored sauces are common. Rice is the primary grain; in addition to being served plain with each meal, it is made into pancakes, dumplings, and fritters. Coconut milk is used instead of cow's milk, coconut cream instead of yogurt. Food is cooked in aromatic spice-infused oils and flavored with curry powder, shallots, and kari leaves.

To the east lie the fertile plains and shores of Bengal, where fish and seafood, mustard in all its forms, squash, and red lentils rule. Stews and stir-fried vegetables are laced with the garlic and panch phoron, a blend of five spices, and tempered with cinnamon and coconut. Fresh coriander, basil, and kari leaves add herbal fragrances.

In the dry regions of western India grow fiber-rich beans and peas, which are cooked with such aromatic spices as ajowan, fennel, and nigella and chiles. Dill and parsley are used as green vegetables. Breads, which are a staple here, are flavored with spices and vegetable purees.

Hindus are the predominant religious group in India. The Jains, Sikhs, and Buddhists, who were once all a part of the Hindu religion, are today distinctly separate communities and form a sizable minority. Together they have laid the foundation of Indian cooking. Their cuisines in their infinite interpretations have come to be known as the regional cooking of India. Of particular importance are two sub-groups: the Hindu Brahmins (one of the four castes of the Hindus) and the Jains. Both are strictly vegetarian, excluding all forms of meat, fish, and their by-products from their diet. Working within their religious taboos and dietary restrictions, these communities have developed a vegetarian cuisine of unparalleled finesse.

Also worth mentioning are those special cultural groups that emerged from foreign influence and whose culinary impact has been profound. Such dishes as the vindaloo of Goa from the Christians of Portuguese descent, shrimp *patia* of Bombay from the Parsis of Persian origin, and kedgeree and foods from the Anglo-Indians are known all over India.

The Muslims are the largest minority group in India. They are credited with introducing the sophisticated Moghul culture to India that gave the world, among other splendors, the Taj Mahal. It was in the royal courts and kitchens of the Moghuls that the most refined of all Indian regional cuisines was born. This style of cooking, with its traces of Persian and Turkish influence, is typified by creamy mellow sauces, subtle fragrances, and exquisite garnishes.

An uncommon array of food exists in India today, ranging from the smoky clay-oven roasted tandoori chicken and *biriyani* pilafs of the Moghuls to the piquant fish curry of the Madras Tamils, from the spice-infused lobster of the Bengalis to the plum-glazed roast duck of the Anglo-Indians. Such dishes represent Indian food in all its intricacies and complexity.

One of the most wonderful aspects of Indian cooking is that complex flavorings are achieved by straightforward cooking techniques. No unfamiliar gadgets need be brought out and mastered. The tools and equipment found in an average Western kitchen, including the food processor and nonstick pans, are more than adequate to perform most of the tasks required in Indian cooking. In other words, Indian cooking is quick and easy, healthy and frugal. All you need to bring to it is a desire to awaken your senses with aromas and flavors.

3

Julie Sahni
New York, 1998

SPICES AND HERBS
IN INDIAN COOKING

INDIAN cooking is the most complexly flavored and the most aromatic of the world's cuisines. This magical property is created by spices and herbs, which are the foundation of Indian cooking. They are used not just to flavor food but to give color, piquancy, heat, and texture to the finished dish. Knowledge of spices and herbs—how they interact with food to bring out the desired flavor—has to be mastered in order to become a natural Indian cook.

In addition to their culinary facet, spices and herbs have medicinal attributes; they are good for the body, mind, and soul. They also act as preservatives, an added benefit since dishes can be prepared ahead and refrigerated for several days without any change in flavor or appearance.

Spices must be cooked in order for them to be digested easily. For this reason spices are always put into a dish at the start of, or at least early in the cooking. When spices are sprinkled over a finished dish such as a yogurt salad or a drink, they must be precooked. This is done by placing the whole spices in a frying pan and toasting them until they turn several shades darker and give off a roasted aroma. Then they are ground.

Spices should be purchased whole (except for ground ginger, cayenne, and turmeric, which are sold in powdered form only) and stored in airtight containers in a cool, dry place. Spices release more fragrance when crushed, so they are generally added to dishes in ground form. To grind spices use a spice mill or coffee grinder reserved for grinding spices or a mortar and pestle. Grind only small quantities of spices as needed, as ground spices quickly go stale.

In India herbs are cultivated all year round and are readily available for use. Both fresh and dried herbs are used in Indian cooking. Fresh herbs, the leaves and the tender stems, are chopped and mixed into dishes or used as a garnish. They may also be chopped and mixed with fresh ginger, spices, and yogurt to serve as relishes and dips, or brewed with fresh ginger and honey in herbal teas. The tradition of using dried herbs began in the mountain regions of northern India where extreme weather conditions prevent year-round herb gardening.

Most spices and herbs used in Indian cooking are widely available. A few of the more unusual, such as ajowan (carum or *ajwain*) or nigella (*kalonji*) can be found in Indian or Pakistani grocery shops or through mail order, but in all cases I have given more readily available alternatives.

Finally, remember that spices and herbs are like perfume: They must be handled with a delicate touch—just enough to tease the palate, leaving behind a trail of exotic intrigue and haunting scents.

Spices and Spice Blends

6

Indian cooks have a way with spices or masalas. In addition to adding them separately during the cooking process, they often premix spices into blends to produce special flavorings; these are also called masalas. They are an intrinsic part of Indian cooking; they lend that special aroma generally associated with a particular dish. Garam Masala is the aroma of tandoori chicken while smoky toasted cumin is that of yogurt salad, for example. The most frequently used prepared spices in Indian kitchen are three spice blends—Curry Powder, Garam Masala, and Panch Phoron. All can be made ahead and stored in a cool, dry place.

Curry Powder

The primary flavor in curry powder is coriander with undertones of fenugreek and turmeric. In the past, the mix contained kari leaf, a fragrant balmy herb, but today it contains only spices. This recipe, one of my favorites, contains fennel, which is used by some communities in South India. It has very little red pepper because I do not like my food fiery-hot. I like to enjoy and appreciate the aromatic aspects of the spices as well as the food. If you want it hot and spicy, add more ground red pepper to your taste.

MAKES ABOUT $^1/_2$ CUP

        3 tablespoons coriander seeds

        2 teaspoons cumin seeds

        1 teaspoon fenugreek seeds

        1 teaspoon fennel seeds

        1 teaspoon yellow mustard seeds

        1 to 2 teaspoons white peppercorns

        6 whole cloves

        2 tablespoons turmeric

        1 to 2 teaspoons ground red pepper

1. Put the coriander, cumin, fenugreek, fennel, mustard seeds, peppercorns, and cloves in a dry heavy skillet over medium heat. Toast the spices, stirring occasionally, until they turn dark brown, about 12 minutes. Do not raise the heat to quicken the process, or the spices will brown prematurely, leaving the insides undercooked. Cool completely.

2. Working in batches if necessary, transfer the mixture to a spice mill or coffee grinder, and grind to a powder. Mix in the turmeric and red pepper. Use immediately or store in an airtight container in a cool, dry place. (*Curry Powder keeps for 3 months.*)

Garam Masala

This is the most aromatic and fragrant of all Indian spice blends. Used throughout North India in all types of dishes—from appetizers and soups to yogurt salad and main courses—this blend is indispensable to Moghul and North Indian cooking. It is widely available, but my homemade version is more fragrant and, of course, fresher.

MAKES ABOUT $^1/_2$ CUP

        2 tablespoons cumin seeds

        2 tablespoons coriander seeds

        2 tablespoons cardamom seeds

7

> 2 tablespoons black peppercorns
>
> 1 piece (3-inches) cinnamon, broken up
>
> 1 teaspoon whole cloves
>
> 1 teaspoon grated nutmeg
>
> 1/2 teaspoon saffron (optional)

1. Put the cumin, coriander, cardamom, pepper, cinnamon and cloves in a heavy skillet over medium-high heat. Toast the spices, stirring occasionally, until they turn several shades darker and give off a sweet smoky aroma, about 10 minutes. Do not raise the heat to quicken the process, or the spices will brown prematurely, leaving the insides undercooked. Cool completely.

2. Working in batches if necessary, transfer the mixture to a spice mill or coffee grinder and grind to a powder. Stir in the nutmeg and saffron, if you are using it. Use immediately or store in an airtight container in a cool, dry place. (*Garam Masala keeps for 3 months.*)

Panch Phoron

A blend of five whole spices—cumin, fennel, mustard, fenugreek, and nigella—Panch Phoron is a Bengal classic. It is used to flavor fish, vegetables, chutneys, and, on occasion, legumes. Although the blend can be assembled at the last minute since there is no roasting involved, I suggest making it ahead if only because measuring spices takes time.

MAKES 1/2 CUP

> 2 tablespoons cumin seeds
>
> 2 tablespoons fennel seeds
>
> 2 tablespoons black mustard seeds
>
> 1 tablespoon fenugreek seeds
>
> 1 tablespoon nigella seeds

Combine all the spices in a jar, cover, and store in a cool, dry place.

Treating a Chile-scorched Mouth

If when eating a highly spiced dish you feel a need to extinguish the fire, reach first for the chilled sweet yogurt drink called *lassi* (page 198). Recent scientific research shows that the lactic acid present in yogurt works best to counter the burn (experienced as pain) in the mouth and throat caused by the chiles. Starchy foods, such as rice or bread, will also work to some extent. One or two swallows followed by a sip of ice water. All these are more efficient than a quaff of beer or wine!

9

THE INDIAN WAY
OF DINING

THE traditional Indian style of eating, *thali,* is somewhat different from what is customary in the West. Various dishes of all the courses are spooned into small individual bowls, which are then neatly arranged on a large (15-inch diameter) rimmed plate or tray. Rice, bread, pickles, and relishes are placed on the plate and this fully arranged *thali* is served to each person. The advantage of this style of serving is that once everyone sits down to eat the meal proceeds without interruption.

It is not necessary, of course, to conform to the *thali* style of eating in order to enjoy an Indian meal. The Western style of serving separate courses is, in fact, very suitable, and I find it avoids the waste often associated with individual servings where it is hard to judge everyone's preferences and capacity.

To compose a simple meal, serve a main dish consisting of meat, poultry, fish, or vegetables and accompany it with bread or rice. For a more elaborate meal, include a selection of side dishes, such as vegetables, *dals,* and salads. Relishes and chutneys are not essential, but they add texture, herbal scent, and bite to the meal.

Finally, there is no reason why these dishes could not be combined with your everyday Western meal. For example, serve the Chicken Curry (page 130) simply with a nice loaf of bread or pita and a green salad, or serve Cauliflower with Nigella in Ginger Oil (page 164) with fried fish. To get you started and make menu planning easier, I have given serving suggestions with each recipe.

Traditional-style Eating with Fingers

Most Indians eat with their fingers, which adds a highly sensual accent to the dining experience. Using fingers, rather than a fork is also logical, especially when bread is served as an accompaniment. Indian breads, like Mexican flour tortillas or Chinese pancakes, are soft and pliable. It is easy to tear a piece and use it to scoop up or wrap around the food.

Sample Menus

Papaya and Potato Salad

Steamed Fish in Herb Sauce

Cumin Potatoes

Lemon Pilaf

Quick Saffron Pudding

Lentil Wafers

Goan Warm Mussel Salad

Nectarine Chutney with Walnuts and Saffron

Chicken Biriyani

Ginger Limeade

Spinach Fritters

Lamb Curry

Cauliflower with Nigella in Ginger Oil

Green Pea Pilaf

Indian Rice Pudding with Cardamom

Mulligatawny

Pan-grilled Scallops with Ajowan

Curry-scented Mushrooms

Semolina Pilaf

Mango Fool

Shrimp Madras

Tandoori Chicken

Broccoli and Carrots in Garlic-Turmeric Oil

Cool Yogurt and Cucumber Salad

Baked Tandoori Bread

Mango Ice Cream

New Delhi Vegetarian Vegetable Soup

Red Kidney Beans with Spicy Sauce

Roasted Pepper and Mint Yogurt Salad

Peach and Walnut Basmati Pilaf

Savory Yogurt Drink with Mint

Bangalore Peanut Soup

Roast Duck with Cinnamon-Plum Glaze

Curried Eggplant with Chutney

Sweet Pumpkin Bread

Spiced Tea

Iced Yogurt Soup With Mint

Spice-rubbed Grilled Lamb

Green Beans in Fenugreek Oil

Deep-fried Puffy Bread

Sweet Mango Lassi

APPETIZERS
AND SOUPS

INDIAN appetizers are delicately flavored morsels with intriguing aromas and complex flavors. These might be spiced nuts, crisp fried wafers, spicy fritters, or a cool salad flavored with smoky roasted cumin. You can also serve stuffed breads or savory pastries or small portions of several main courses, including tandoori meats and vegetables, as appetizers.

Although India does not have a tradition of serving soup as a first course, there are many soupy preparations that are served as a one-dish meal or as a part of the meal. Both chilled and hot soups, totally vegetarian or made with chunks of fish, chicken, or lamb, are popular. These soups are light and fragrant and stimulate the appetite.

A great thing about these appetizers and soups is that they can be made in advance and briefly heated before serving. Most of them also freeze well. Just remember to serve them all in small portions as they are meant to awaken rather than satisfy the appetite.

BENGAL FISH BALLS
with Scallions

Machi Kofta

A specialty of Bangladesh, these little balls are delicious served as an appetizer with a dipping sauce such as Mint Chutney (page 189). They also make a fine light meal accompanied by a salad.

SERVES 6

3/4 pound skinless and boneless sole, flounder, scrod, or haddock fillets, poached and flaked

1 pound potatoes, boiled, peeled, and coarsely mashed

1/4 cup plain yogurt

1/2 cup thinly sliced scallions, both white and green parts

1 tablespoon finely chopped fresh ginger

2 teaspoons lemon juice

1 tablespoon Curry Powder (page 6)

2 teaspoons dry mustard

1 teaspoon coarse salt or to taste

Peanut or corn oil, for deep-frying

1. Combine all the ingredients except the oil in a bowl and mix well. Pick up the mixture in 1-tablespoonful amounts and roll into neat balls. You should have about 36 balls.

2. Pour the oil into a *kadhai* or deep-fryer to a depth of 2 inches. Heat over medium-high heat to 375°. When the oil is hot, slip in a few balls at a time, making sure not to overcrowd the pan. Fry the balls, turning, until golden brown and crisp all around, about 4 minutes. Using a slotted spoon, remove and drain on paper towels. (*The balls may be made ahead and refrigerated for up to 4 hours. To reheat, drop them into hot oil for 45 seconds and serve. Or reheat in a 325° oven for 7 minutes.*)

3. Serve immediately.

Variation:

Cooked minced shrimp, scallops, or chicken breast meat may be used instead of the fish.

19

SHRIMP MADRAS

Jheenga Chat

Here is a wonderful recipe of the chettinad *(the business community) of Madras whose food often reflects a fusion of northern and southern flavors. In this shrimp preparation, for example, both Curry Powder and* Garam Masala *are used to achieve intriguingly complex results.*

SERVES 4

1 1/2 pounds jumbo or large shrimp, peeled, deveined, and rinsed

1 teaspoon Curry Powder (page 6)

1 teaspoon *Garam Masala* (page 7)

24 fresh kari leaves, cut into chiffonade; or 1 tablespoon dried kari leaves, coarsely powdered

1 teaspoon minced garlic

1 tablespoon vegetable oil

1 tablespoon tomato paste

1/4 cup coconut milk, fresh (see page 211) or canned

Coarse salt to taste

1 tablespoon lemon juice

1 bunch (6 to 7 ounces) watercress, trimmed, rinsed, and patted dry

1. Place the shrimp in a bowl. Add the Curry Powder, *Garam Masala*, kari leaves, garlic, and oil and crumble over the shrimps.

2. Heat a frying pan over high heat until very hot. Add the shrimps and sear, shaking and tossing, for 1 minute, or until they begin to turn pink and curl up. Whisk the tomato paste into the coconut milk and add to the shrimps. Continue to cook until the sauce is reduced to a glaze and the shrimps are cooked through, about 5 minutes. Sprinkle with salt and lemon juice and turn off the heat.

3. Spread the watercress on a plate and mound the shrimps on top of it. Serve immediately.

21

Spicy Almonds

Bhone Badaam

Beware: *These addictive nibbles go very fast and can easily ruin the appetite for good things to come. In this recipe the heat is moderate. For a spicier version, increase the ground red pepper to two teaspoons.*

Serves 8

> 2 teaspoons ground cumin
>
> 2 teaspoons ground red pepper
>
> 1 teaspoon coarse salt or to taste
>
> $^1/_2$ cup vegetable oil
>
> 16 ounces (about 3 cups) whole unblanched almonds
>
> $^1/_4$ cup sugar
>
> 2 teaspoons lemon juice

1. Combine the cumin, red pepper, and salt in a small bowl. Set aside.

2. Heat the oil over medium heat in a *kadhai* or large skillet. Add the almonds and fry, stirring constantly, until the nuts are puffed and give off a roasted fragrance, about 5 minutes. Do not overfry, or they will taste burned. Drain the nuts in a sieve and set aside.

3. Heat $^1/_4$ cup of water with the lemon juice and sugar in a small pot over medium heat until the sugar is fully dissolved. Increase the heat and boil the syrup rapidly for 3 minutes. Turn off the heat. Add the nuts and mix well to coat. Spread the nuts in a single layer on a cookie sheet. Immediately sprinkle them with the spice mixture, turning to coat evenly.

4. Cool completely before serving.

Curry Powder spices (clockwise from bottom): coriander seeds, turmeric, cloves, ground red pepper, fennel seeds, fenugreek seeds, white peppercorns, cumin seeds

Garam Masala spices (clockwise from upper right): coriander seeds, cardamom seeds, black peppercorns, cinnamon sticks, cardamom pods, cloves, saffron; nutmeg in center

Lentil Wafers in cumin, garlic, green chile, and black pepper flavors BELOW (from right to left): **Coconut Chutney, Mint Chutney, Spinach Fritters,** and **Savory Pastries with Spicy Chicken Filling**

Three puffy breads (clockwise from the right): **Sweet Pumpkin Bread, Green Pea Bread,** and **Deep Fried Puffy Bread**

Peach and Walnut
Basmati Pilaf and
Sweet Mango Lassi

Tandoori Chicken and
Cool Cucumber and Yogurt Salad

**Spice-rubbed Grilled Lamb
and Saffron Pilaf**

Steamed Fish in Herb Sauce and **Lemon Pilaf**

Goan Warm Mussel Salad

LENTIL WAFERS

Puppadum/Papad

These ready-made dried lentil wafers come in such flavors as garlic, black pepper, and cumin. All you need to do is dip them in hot oil; they will puff up and cook in a matter of seconds. Two or three per person is a good portion size.

SERVES 8

> Peanut or corn oil, for deep-frying
>
> 1 package storebought *puppadum/papad*

1. Pour the oil into a *kadhai* or a deep-fryer to a depth of 2 inches. Heat over medium-high heat to 375°.

2. When the oil is hot, slip 1 wafer into the oil. Fry for about 5 seconds, or until the wafer turns several shades lighter and expands considerably. Remove with tongs and drain on paper towels. Fry all the wafers the same way.

3. Serve immediately.

NOTE: The *puppadum* can also be baked in a preheated 425° oven for 6 minutes or in the microwave on high for 50 seconds.

23

CAULIFLOWER AND PEANUT FRITTERS

Gobhi Pakora

Crunchy and studded with peanuts, these cauliflower fritters are popular with all age groups. The fritters are great served with a yogurt salad or chutney as a dipping sauce

SERVES 4

1 medium head cauliflower (about 1 1/2 pounds)
Peanut or corn oil, for deep-frying

CHICK-PEA BATTER

1 cup chick-pea flour

1/2 cup finely chopped peanuts

1/2 cup chopped fresh coriander (cilantro)
    leaves and tender stems

1 tablespoon ground coriander

1/2 teaspoon cracked black peppercorns

1 tablespoon peanut or corn oil

1/2 cup water

1/2 teaspoon baking powder

Coarse salt to taste

24

1. Trim the cauliflower and cut into florets. Pour the oil into a *kadhai* or a deep-fryer to a depth of 2$\frac{1}{2}$ inches. Heat over medium-high heat to 375°.

2. Combine all the ingredients for the batter in a large bowl and mix thoroughly to make a smooth batter. Add the cauliflower florets, turning to coat evenly.

3. Add the cauliflower, a few pieces at a time, to the hot oil. Do not overcrowd the pan. Fry until the coating is golden brown, turning occasionally, about 6 minutes. Drain on paper towels. (*The fritters may be made ahead and refrigerated for up to 1 day or frozen. Defrost frozen fritters before refrying. Reheat the fritters in hot oil for 30 seconds and serve or reheat frozen fritters in a 375° oven for 10 minutes.*)

4. Serve immediately.

Variation:

Substitute the same amount of broccoli, trimmed, peeled, and cut into 1-inch pieces, for the cauliflower.

25

FRAGRANT ONION
and Zucchini Fritters

Piaz Ghia Pakora

These fritters, scented with cumin and coriander, are a popular North Indian snack. They are excellent served with drinks or afternoon tea. Their versatile flavor makes it possible to serve them before any main dish.

SERVES 4

Peanut or corn oil, for deep-frying

4 medium onions, peeled and thinly sliced

1 small zucchini, grated

1 cup (lightly packed) fresh coriander (cilantro) leaves and tender stems

1/4 cup yogurt

1 cup chick-pea flour or all-purpose flour

2 teaspoons ground cumin

1/2 teaspoon ground red pepper

1 teaspoon baking powder

Coarse salt to taste

1. Pour the oil into a *kadhai* or deep-fryer to a depth of 2 inches. Heat over medium heat to 375°.

2. Put all the remaining ingredients in a bowl and mix until the vegetables are evenly coated. Gently drop the batter mixture, in 2-tablespoonful amounts, into the oil. Make only a few fritters at a time, so that there is ample room for them to float easily in the oil. Fry the fritters, turning them until they are golden brown all over, 8 to 10 minutes. Using a slotted spoon, remove the fritters and drain on paper towels. (*The fritters may be made ahead and refrigerated for up to 1 day or frozen. Defrost frozen fritters before refrying. Reheat the fritters in hot oil for 30 seconds or reheat frozen fritters in a 375° oven for 10 minutes.*)

3. Serve immediately.

Variation:

Substitute 8 ounces asparagus, trimmed, peeled, and sliced into 1-inch pieces for the zucchini.

27

POTATO AND EGGPLANT FRITTERS

Aloo Pakora

These fritters are popular throughout India, where the flavoring varies from region to region. In North India, for example, Garam Masala is a favorite flavoring while Curry Powder is more common in the south. Follow these spicy fritters with an earthy and smoky dish like Tandoori Chicken (page 90)

SERVES 4

> 3/4 pound small waxy new potatoes
>
> 1 small eggplant (about 3/4 pound)

BATTER

> 1 1/2 cups chick-pea flour
>
> 1 tablespoon vegetable oil
>
> 1 cup water
>
> 1 tablespoon lemon juice
>
> 1 tablespoon *Garam Masala* (page 7)
>   or Curry Powder (page 6)
>
> 1 teaspoon coarse salt or to taste
>
> 1 teaspoon baking soda
>
> Peanut or corn oil, for deep-frying

28

1. Scrub the potatoes and cut them into $1/8$-inch-thick rounds. Quarter the egg-plant lengthwise and cut it crosswise into $1/4$-inch-thick slices. Put the vegetables in a bowl of water and set aside.

2. Combine all the ingredients for the batter in a large bowl and mix thoroughly to make a smooth batter.

3. Pour the oil into a *kadhai* or a deep-fryer to a depth of $2^1/_2$ inches. Heat over medium-high heat to 375°.

4. Drain the vegetables and lightly pat dry on paper towels. Dip the vegetables into the batter and gently drop into the oil. Make only a few fritters at a time, so that there is ample room for them to float easily in the oil. Fry, turning frequently, until the coating is golden brown, about 7 minutes. Drain on paper towels.

5. Serve immediately.

Variation:

Substitute a 2-pound cauliflower cut into small florets for the potato and eggplant.

SPINACH FRITTERS

Palak Pakora

Another excellent cocktail-hour nibble, these fritters are lovely made with leaf spinach. Serve them with Nectarine Chutney with Walnuts and Saffron (page 195).

SERVES 4

8 ounces leaf spinach

BATTER

1 cup chick-pea flour

1 tablespoon vegetable oil

$^2/_3$ cup water

1 teaspoon minced garlic

2 teaspoons ground coriander

1 teaspoon cumin seeds

$^1/_2$ teaspoon red pepper flakes

$^1/_2$ teaspoon baking powder

1 teaspoon coarse salt or to taste

Peanut or corn oil, for deep-frying

1. Trim and wash the spinach thoroughly and cut any large leaves in half. Combine all the ingredients for the batter in a large bowl and mix thoroughly to make a smooth batter.

2. Pour the oil into a *kadhai* or deep-fryer to a depth of 2^1/$_2$ inches. Heat over medium-high heat to 375°.

3. When the oil is hot, add the spinach, a few leaves at a time, to the batter, mix to coat, and drop into the hot oil. Do not overcrowd the pan. Fry until golden brown, about 3 minutes. Drain on paper towels

4. Serve immediately.

Variation:

Other greens, such as watercress, arugula, mustard, or kale, may be substituted for the spinach.

PAPAYA AND POTATO SALAD

Papeeta Aloo Chat

A New Delhi specialty, papaya chat is one of my favorite appetizers. For a more sub-stantial salad, fold in eight ounces of cooked chicken, fish, shrimp, or crabmeat. The spices and salt make the fruit sweat, so for best results assemble the chat just before serving.

SERVES 4

1 ripe papaya

1 pound potatoes, boiled, peeled, and cut into
   $^1/_4$-inch slices

1 tablespoon maple syrup or honey

$^1/_4$ cup lemon juice

Coarse salt to taste

2 teaspoons ground toasted cumin seeds

$^1/_4$ cup finely chopped mint leaves

$^1/_2$ cup finely chopped fresh coriander (cilantro)
   leaves and tender stems

4 green chiles, seeded and sliced

4 lettuce leaves

32

1. Cut the papaya in half, scoop out the seeds and peel carefully. Cut each half into 1-inch wedges and put in a bowl. Add the other ingredients except the lettuce leaves and toss well.

2. Arrange the salad on the lettuce leaves on individual plates and serve.

Variations:

Substitute other seasonal fruit for the papaya, such as peaches, apricots, apples, bananas, kiwifruit, and slightly unripe mangoes, or a combination. Or substitute 1 medium green bell pepper and 1 medium red bell pepper, seeded and cut into 1-inch squares, for the potatoes and omit the green chiles.

MULLIGATAWNY

Molahatanni

Mulligatawny, a curried meat and vegetable soup, originated in the British Raj. There are as many interpretations of this soup as there are cooks in India. This one is from the Planter's Club in Ootacamund, a small town in southern India. Depending upon how spicy you want the soup to be, add more or less ground red pepper.

SERVES 8

$1/3$ cup yellow split peas (see Note)

1 cup chopped carrot

1 cup chopped zucchini

1 cup chopped potato

1 tablespoon chopped fresh ginger

$3^{1}/_{2}$ cups Chicken Stock (recipe follows)

$2^{1}/_{2}$ cups finely chopped onions

1 cup (lightly packed) chopped fresh coriander
    (cilantro) leaves and tender stems

3 tablespoons *usli ghee* (page 216) or clarified
    butter

1 tablespoon finely chopped garlic

$1/2$ teaspoon ground red pepper

2 tablespoons Curry Powder (page 6)

$1/2$ cup heavy or light cream, or milk

1 cup chopped cooked chicken (optional)

Coarse salt and black pepper

1. Pick over the split peas, discarding any shriveled ones or pebbles, rinse, and drain. Put the peas, carrot, zucchini, potato, ginger, stock, 1 cup of the onion and $^1/_2$ cup of the coriander in a deep pot and place over high heat. Bring to a boil. Lower the heat and simmer, covered, for 45 minutes or until the peas are very tender. Let cool. Purée the soup in batches using a blender or food processor. Return the soup to the pot and reheat.

2. Meanwhile, heat the *usli ghee* in a frying pan over medium-high heat. Add the remaining onion, the garlic, red pepper, and Curry Powder. Cook, stirring constantly, until the onion is lightly fried, about 6 minutes. Pour the contents of the frying pan into the soup. Stir in the cream, and chicken (if using), and season with salt and pepper.

3. When piping hot, ladle into individual soup bowls. Garnish with the remaining coriander, if using. Serve immediately.

NOTE: While it's preferable to use Indian yellow split peas, the dried yellow peas available in supermarkets can be substituted.

Variation: ───────────────────────────────

Substitute any cooked seafood, such as crabmeat or lobster, for the chicken.

35

CHICKEN STOCK

Yakhni

Indian chicken stock is highly fragrant, with cumin, fresh ginger, garlic, and cilantro. The stock is wonderful in soups, pilafs, and curries. It is fairly simple to make: all you do is boil bones in the aromatic liquid. For a spicier stock add chopped hot green chile to the liquid.

MAKES ABOUT 4 CUPS

> 4 cups chicken, hen, duck, or turkey bones,
>   lightly cracked
>
> 6 cups water
>
> 1 teaspoon cumin seeds
>
> 4 cloves garlic, roughly sliced
>
> $1/2$ inch piece fresh ginger
>
> 1 cup (lightly packed) fresh coriander (cilantro)
>   leaves and tender stems

1. Combine all the ingredients in a deep pot and bring to a boil over high heat. Lower the heat and simmer, uncovered, for 2 hours. Turn off the heat. When cool, strain the stock and use or store in 2-pint containers.

NOTE: The stock keeps for 3 days in the refrigerator or up to 3 months in the freezer.

INDIAN CHICKEN SOUP

Murgh Shorva

From the Muslim community in northwestern India, this piquant soup is particularly welcome on a cool winter day. If desired, serve it with crackers alongside.

SERVES 8

> 1 chicken (3 pounds), quartered
>
> 4 tablespoons *usli ghee* (see page 216)
>   or vegetable oil
>
> 1 tablespoon thinly sliced garlic
>
> 2 tablespoons julienned fresh ginger
>
> 2 teaspoons *Garam Masala* (page 7)
>   or ground cumin
>
> 2 bay leaves
>
> 1½ cups thinly sliced onion
>
> 3 lemon slices
>
> 2 tablespoons finely chopped mint
>
> Coarse salt and black pepper
>
> 1 whole lemon, halved

1. Rinse the chicken and pat it dry. Place a heavy, deep pot over medium-high heat and add the *usli ghee* and chicken. Cook until the chicken is lightly seared, about 5 minutes. Add the garlic, ginger, *Garam Masala*, bay leaves, onion, and lemon. Cook until the spices give off an aroma.

2. Add 8 cups water and bring to a boil. Skim off the scum as it rises to the top. Lower the heat and simmer, partially covered, for 2 to 6 hours (the longer the soup simmers the richer the flavor will be). Add more water as necessary during cooking. Strain the soup and discard the solids. Stir in the mint and salt and pepper to taste. Add a squeeze of lemon juice to taste.

3. Serve piping hot in mugs.

37

BANGALORE PEANUT SOUP

Moongphali Shorva

This delicate soup, rich with sweet creamy peanuts and herbal coriander, comes from Bangalore, hometown of the Anglo-Indians.

SERVES 6

2 tablespoons *usli ghee* (see page 216)
    or clarified butter

1 tablespoon ground coriander

$^1/_2$ teaspoon turmeric

1 teaspoon minced garlic

1 $^1/_2$ cups finely chopped onion

1 teaspoon ground ginger

4 cups Chicken Stock, homemade
    (see page 36) or canned

$^1/_2$ cup creamy peanut butter

1 tablespoon sesame paste (optional)

3 tablespoons cornstarch dissolved in
    $^1/_4$ cup water

$^1/_3$ cup heavy or light cream, or milk

Coarse salt and black pepper

2 tablespoons lime juice

Chopped roasted peanuts, chopped scallions,
    chopped fresh coriander (cilantro) leaves
    and minced green chiles, for garnish

1. Heat the *usli ghee* in a deep pot. Add the coriander, turmeric, garlic, onion, and ginger. Cook until the onions are lightly fried, about 6 minutes. Add the stock, peanut butter, and sesame paste, if using, and bring to a boil. Lower the heat and simmer for 5 minutes.

2. Add the cornstarch mixture and cook, stirring constantly, until the soup thickens, about 2 minutes. Stir in the cream, salt, and a liberal grinding of pepper. Heat until piping hot.

3. Add the lime juice, garnish with peanuts, scallions, fresh coriander, and chiles, and serve.

39

NEW DELHI
Vegetarian Vegetable Soup

Sabzi Shorva

A popular dish from the Indian capital, this soup is bursting with the flavor of garden-fresh vegetables. It makes a light meal with bread and salad. The soup traditionally has a glowing hot flavor due to the addition of ground hot pepper. For a milder flavor reduce or eliminate the red pepper.

SERVES 6

> 1 medium head cauliflower (about 2 pounds)
>
> 2 medium potatoes, peeled and diced
>
> 2 cups chopped peeled tomatoes,
>   fresh or canned
>
> 1 teaspoon turmeric
>
> 1/2 teaspoon ground red pepper
>
> 2 tablespoons vegetable oil
>
> 1 teaspoon cumin seeds
>
> 1 cup frozen peas
>
> Coarse salt and black pepper
>
> 1/2 cup chopped (lightly packed) fresh coriander
>   (cilantro) leaves and tender stems

1. Trim the cauliflower and cut it into florets. Peel the stems and cut them into small pieces. Combine the cauliflower, potatoes, tomatoes, turmeric, and red pepper in a bowl.

2. Heat the oil in a deep pot over medium-high heat. Add the cumin and cook until the seeds turn dark brown. Add the vegetable-spice mixture and 3 cups water. Bring to a boil. Lower the heat and simmer, covered, until the vegetables are tender, about 30 minutes. Add the frozen peas during the last 10 minutes of cooking. Season with salt and black pepper.

3. Sprinkle with the chopped coriander and serve.

40

ICED YOGURT SOUP .
with Mint

Dahi Shorva

An uncommonly refreshing soup to beat the heat. It is simple and quick to make on hot summer days.

SERVES 4

2 cups yogurt

1 cup buttermilk

$1/4$ cup ice water

2 teaspoons honey or sugar

$1/2$ teaspoon coarse salt

1 teaspoon ground toasted cumin seeds
  (see page 212)

2 tablespoons minced mint

1 cup grated cucumber, drained

$1/2$ cup finely diced red bell pepper

$1/4$ cup thinly sliced scallions, white and
  green parts

$1/2$ cup toasted chopped walnuts or cashews

Mint sprigs, for garnish

1. Whisk together the yogurt, buttermilk, ice water, honey, salt, cumin, mint, cucumber, bell pepper, and scallions in a large bowl. Transfer to a chilled soup tureen.

2. Sprinkle with walnuts, garnish with mint sprigs, and serve.

41

BREADS AND
SAVORY PASTRIES

Second only to Tandoori Chicken, Indian breads are the most popular item on an Indian restaurant menu. Made with whole wheat flour and sometimes flavored with spices, herbs, and vegetable purees, these breads are very satisfying. Most are unleavened flatbreads that are easy and quick to make. Those familiar with the Mexican tortilla will find a striking resemblance, except that everyday Indian breads are lighter since they are made with no fat or oil.

All breads may be made ahead and set aside at room temperature or refrigerated until needed, depending on the bread. To reheat, place on a hot frying pan for a few minutes, one at a time. Or heat the entire batch in a preheated 400° oven for 4 minutes or in the microwave for 40 seconds.

43

GRIDDLE-BAKED FLATBREAD

Chapati

Chapati, *a wholesome and earthy-tasting whole wheat bread, is a staple of North India. Chapatis are similar to flour tortillas except these breads are always made with whole grain flour with the bran and germ intact. The soft and pliable chapati is made by rolling out the dough into a thin round disk and baking it on a hot griddle. Chapati goes well with all dishes.*

SERVES 4 TO 6

MAKES 12 CHAPATIS

> 1 1/2 cups *chapati* flour or 3/4 cup whole wheat
> flour and 3/4 cup unbleached all-purpose
> flour, plus additional flour for dusting
>
> 1/2 cup warm water
>
> 3 tablespoons *usli ghee* (see page 216)
> or clarified butter (optional)

1. Put the flour in a large bowl. If using whole wheat and all-purpose flour, stir briefly to combine. Pour the water and 1 tablespoon of the *usli ghee*, if using, over the flour. Mix thoroughly until the flour sticks together. Transfer the dough to a lightly floured surface and knead for 3 minutes. Cover the dough and let it rest for 15 minutes. To make the dough in a food processor, put the flour in the workbowl. If using whole wheat and all-purpose flour, run the machine briefly to combine. With the machine running, add the water-fat mixture through the feed tube and mix until a ball of dough forms on the blade. Process for 50 seconds to knead. (*The dough may be prepared ahead and set aside at room temperature for up to 8 hours or refrigerated for 5 days. Bring the dough to room temperature before using.*)

2. Shape the dough into a rope and cut it into 12 equal portions. Shape each portion into a smooth ball and roll out into a circle, dusting often with flour to prevent sticking. Cover the rounds with a moist towel as you complete rolling them. Do not stack them.

3. Heat a griddle or a frying pan over medium-high heat until very hot. Working with one at a time, place a round on the hot griddle. Bake for $1^1/_2$ to 2 minutes or until brown spots appear on the underside. Turn the bread using tongs and continue to bake for 1 minute more, or until the second side is cooked through the same way. Remove and brush lightly with the remaining *usli ghee*, if desired.

4. Serve immediately or keep warm, covered, in a low oven.

45

FLAME-ROASTED PUFFY BREAD

Phulka

In the North Indian Language, phulka *means puffed, which what these balloonlike breads are. Here,* chapatis *(see page 44) are double-baked by being toasted over a gas flame or on an electric burner. If you use an electric burner, place a cake rack flat on the burner and turn the temperature to the highest level. You can also toast the breads by placing them briefly on the rack of a preheated charcoal or electric grill.*

SERVES 4 TO 6

MAKES 12 *PHULKAS*

> 1 recipe *chapati* (see page 44)
>
> 3 tablespoons *usli ghee* (see page 216)
> or clarified butter (optional)

46

1. Make the *chapatis* through Step 3 as directed on page 44.

2. Pick up a bread with tongs and place it directly over a gas flame or an electric burner. Toast the bread briefly until it is lightly spotted with brown and puffs into a pillow. Turn the bread a few times to ensure even browning and prevent it from burning.

3. Drizzle *usli ghee* on top, if desired, and serve immediately.

NOTE: These breads are meant to be eaten as soon as they are baked; keeping deflates them.

BAKED TANDOORI BREAD

Nan

Nan is the popular bread generally served in Indian restaurants. It is the obvious choice to accompany tandoori meat, chicken, or vegetables (see chapter on Tandoori Grilling) because it is baked in the tandoor, *the Indian clay oven, after the meat.*

SERVES 8

MAKES 8 NANS

1/2 cup yogurt

3/4 cup boiling water

1 teaspoon active dry yeast

2 teaspoons sugar

3/4 teaspoon coarse salt

1/4 melted unsalted butter, plus additional
melted butter for brushing

1 large egg

3 cups unbleached all-purpose flour,
plus additional for dusting

Vegetable oil as needed

1. Whisk together the yogurt and water in a large bowl. Add the yeast, sugar, salt, butter, and egg and mix thoroughly. Add the flour and mix just until a dough forms (the dough will be very soft and sticky). Wipe your hands clean and oil them generously. Knead the dough in the bowl until smooth and satiny, oiling your fingers if necessary, about 10 minutes. Cover and let the dough rest in a warm place for 4 hours, or until doubled in bulk.

2. Preheat the oven to 500°.

3. Punch down the dough first, then knead again for 1 minute. Divide the dough into 8 equal portions and roll out each into a 5-inch round. Using your hands, stretch the round into a 5- to 7-inch oval. Arrange in a single layer on baking sheets and bake in the middle level of the oven for 4 1/2 minutes, or until they begin to puff and brown. Remove and, if desired, grill the *nans* briefly, 15 to 20 seconds, to brown nicely. Brush them with additional melted butter.

4. Arrange the *nan* in a small basket and serve immediately.

49

GREEN CHILE-CORN BREAD

Molahadu

This fragrant bread, imbued with sweetness of corn and accented with slivers of green chiles, is a specialty of the Guntur chile pickers, one of the many migrant groups of southern India. Made with pureed fresh corn, cumin seeds, and chiles, it makes an incredibly satisfying meal when served with a chutney, like Peach Chutney with Walnut and Saffron (page 194) or Garlic Tomato Chutney (page 191). Molahadu is also great with tandoori grilled dishes.

SERVES 6

MAKES 8 MOLAHADUS

> 1 3/4 cups *chapati* flour or 3/4 cup whole wheat
>   flour and 1 cup unbleached all-purpose
>   flour, plus additional flour for dusting
>
> 1 1/2 cups corn kernels, fresh or frozen
>   and thawed
>
> 1/3 cup shredded mild or hot green chiles
>
> 1 teaspoon cumin seeds
>
> Coarse salt
>
> 6 tablespoon *usli ghee* (see page 216)
>   or vegetable oil

1. Put the flour in a large bowl. If using whole wheat and all-purpose flour, stir briefly to combine. Add the corn, chiles, cumin, and salt to taste. Blend the mixture until it forms a firm, kneadable mass. Add 2 tablespoons of the *usli ghee*, and water, as necessary, and knead the dough for 1 minute.

2. Divide the dough into 8 equal portions and shape each into a smooth ball. Roll each ball into a 6-inch round, dusting often with flour to prevent sticking.

3. Heat a griddle or heavy frying pan over high heat. Lower the heat to medium-high and place 1 bread on the griddle. Cook until the underside is spotted with brown, about 2 minutes. Turn and cook until the second side is spotted with brown and the bread is cooked through, about 1 minute.

4. Brush the top of each round with the *usli ghee*, flip, and cook for about 1 minute. Then coat the other side with *usli ghee*, flip, and cook for another minute. Remove and keep warm, covered, while you cook the remaining rounds.

5. Serve immediately.

NOTE: For an intense roasted-corn flavor, after cooking the bread on the griddle (step 3), hold it directly over a high flame for few seconds, using tongs, and toast, turning frequently. Do not let it burn. Brush generously with *usli ghee* and serve.

DEEP-FRIED PUFFY BREAD

Poori

A poori looks like a balloon. The bread is made by dropping rolled-out rounds of dough into hot oil where they undergo a metamorphosis, magically reappearing as light, airy puffs of bread. Pooris are also called show-off breads because they look and taste so sensational. Naturally they are the bread of choice for entertaining. While pooris go well with just about every dish, they seem to have a particular affinity to potatoes; try them with Cumin Potatoes (page 169).

SERVES 4

MAKES 8 *POORIS*

> ¹/₂ cup *chapati* flour or unbleached all-purpose
>   flour, plus additional for dusting
>
> ¹/₂ cup self-rising flour
>
> ¹/₃ cup buttermilk
>
> Peanut or corn oil, for deep-frying

1. Combine the *chapati* and self-rising flour in a medium bowl. Mix in the buttermilk. Knead the dough on a lightly floured surface for 2 minutes. Cover and let rest for 15 minutes. To make the dough in a food processor, put both flours in the workbowl and run the machine until they are blended. With the machine running, add the buttermilk through the feed tube and mix until a ball of dough forms on the blade. Process the dough for 30 seconds, turning the machine on and off every 5 seconds. Remove the dough to the work surface and keep covered with a moist towel.

2. Divide the dough into 8 pieces. Take 1 piece and shape it into a smooth ball. Dust generously with flour and roll into a 5-inch circle. Cover and repeat with the remaining pieces of dough. Do not stack the rounds.

3. Pour the oil into a *kadhai* or deep-fryer to a depth of 4 inches and heat to 375°. Add 1 round to the oil; it will sink to the bottom. When it starts to rise, gently press it in the center with the back of a slotted spoon until the bread puffs. Turn and cook until lightly browned, about 20 seconds. Using a slotted spoon, transfer to paper towels. The *poori* will be light and puffed up, just like a balloon. Keep warm while cooking the remaining *pooris*.

4. Place on a platter and serve immediately.

GREEN PEA BREAD

Hari Poori

Another classic bread from North India, Green Pea Bread is loved by grown-ups and children alike. This emerald green poori is made by enriching the dough with pureed green peas and fresh coriander (cilantro). I like to add a little ground black pepper, which seems to bring out the herbal flavor of the peas.

SERVES 4

MAKES 8 *POORIS*

> $^1/_2$ cup frozen green peas, thawed
>
> $^1/_2$ cup (lightly packed) fresh coriander (cilantro) leaves and tender stems
>
> 1 cup unbleached all-purpose flour, plus additional for dusting
>
> Coarse salt and black pepper to taste
>
> Peanut or corn oil, for deep-frying

54

1. Put the green peas and coriander into the workbowl of a food processor and process for 30 seconds, or until the peas are pureed. Add the flour, salt, pepper, and 1 tablespoon oil and process until well blended. With the machine running, add $1/4$ cup of water through the feed tube, mixing until a ball of dough forms on the blade. Process the dough for 30 seconds, turning the machine on and off every 5 seconds. Remove the dough to a lightly floured surface and keep covered with a moist towel.

2. Divide the dough in half. Shape each half into a rope and cut into 4 equal portions. Cover with a moist towel. Shape each portion of dough into a smooth ball and roll out into a 3-inch circle, dusting often with flour to prevent sticking. Cover and repeat with the remaining pieces of dough. Do not stack the *pooris*.

3. Pour the oil in a *kadhai* or deep-fryer to a depth of 3 inches and heat to 375°. Add 1 *poori* to the oil; it will sink to the bottom. When it starts to rise, gently press it to the center of the pan with the back of a slotted spoon until the bread puffs, about 30 seconds. Turn and cook until lightly browned, about 15 seconds. Using the slotted spoon, transfer the *poori* to paper towels. The bread will be light and puffed up, just like a balloon. Keep it in a warm oven while cooking the remaining breads.

4. Mound the *poori* in a large shallow basket and serve immediately.

Variation:

Substitute an equal amount of cooked and puréed lima beans or green split peas for the green peas.

55

SWEET PUMPKIN BREAD

Lal Poori

I grew up eating pooris like this that were flavored with puréed vegetables. They are lovely by themselves with a cup of coffee; they also go nicely with chicken and meat curries.

SERVES 8

MAKES 16 *POORIS*

> 1 cup pureed cooked pumpkin, fresh or canned
>
> ¹/₂ teaspoon *Garam Masala* (page 7) or ground cinnamon
>
> 1 tablespoon peanut or corn oil
>
> 2¹/₄ cups *chapati* flour or unbleached all-purpose flour, plus additional for dusting
>
> Peanut or corn oil, for deep-frying

1. Put the pumpkin, *Garam Masala*, oil, and flour in a large bowl and mix well. Add enough water to make the mixture come together in a nonsticky, kneadable dough. Gather the dough together and knead it until smooth, dusting with flour if it is very sticky. To make the dough in a food processor, put the pumpkin, *Garam Masala*, oil, and flour in the workbowl and run the machine until well blended. With the machine running, add the water through the feed tube and mix until a ball of dough forms on the blade. Process the dough for 30 seconds, turning the machine on and off every 5 seconds. Remove the dough to a lightly floured surface and keep covered with a moist towel.

2. Divide the dough in half. Shape each half into a rope and cut into 8 equal portions. Cover with a moist towel. Shape each portion of dough into a smooth ball and roll into a 3-inch circle, dusting often with flour to prevent sticking. Cover and repeat with the remaining pieces of dough. Do not stack the *pooris*.

3. Pour the oil in a *kadhai* or deep-fryer to a depth of 3 inches. Heat the oil to 375°. Add 1 poori to the oil; it will sink to the bottom. When it starts to rise, gently press it in the center with the back of a slotted spoon until the bread puffs, about 30 seconds. Turn and cook until lightly browned, about 15 seconds. Using a slotted spoon, transfer to paper towels. The bread will be light and puffed up, just like a balloon. Keep warm while cooking the remaining breads.

4. Mound the *pooris* in a large shallow basket and serve immediately.

Variation:

Substitute an equal amount of mashed potato, sweet potato, or turnip for the pumpkin.

57

FLAKY PARSLEY PINWHEEL BREAD

Saag Paratha

Flavored with the highly aromatic parsley called bandhana, *this bread is among my favorites. In the western province of Punjab in North India, where this bread comes from, parsley is used not as a seasoning herb but as a green much the way spinach, mustard, and swiss chard are used. Cut into wedges, parsley bread makes an excellent appetizer with before-dinner drinks. It also goes well with tandoori grilled meats.*

SERVES 4 TO 8

MAKES 8 *PARATHAS*

> 1 1/2 cups *chapati* flour or 3/4 cup whole wheat
> flour and 3/4 cup unbleached all-purpose
> flour, plus additional flour for dusting
>
> 1/2 teaspoon nigella or fennel seeds
>
> 1/2 teaspoon coarse salt
>
> 1/4 cup *usli ghee* (see page 216) or vegetable oil
>
> 1/2 cup warm water
>
> 2 cups (lightly packed) parsley leaves, minced

1. Put the flour in a large bowl. If using whole wheat and all-purpose flour, stir briefly to combine. Add the nigella, salt, and 1 tablespoon of the *usli ghee*. Add the water and mix until the flour comes together into a nonsticky, kneadable dough. Transfer the dough to a lightly floured work surface and knead for 3 minutes. Cover the dough and let it rest for 15 minutes. To make the dough in a food processor, put the flour in the workbowl. If using whole wheat and all-purpose flour, run the machine briefly to combine. Add the nigella, salt, and 1 tablespoon of the *usli ghee*. With the machine running, add the water through the feed tube and mix until a ball of dough forms on the blade. Process for 50 seconds to knead. (*The dough may be prepared ahead and set aside at room temperature for up to 8 hours or refrigerated for 2 days. Bring the dough to room temperature before using.*)

2. Shape the dough into a ball and roll out into an 8-inch circle, dusting often with flour to prevent sticking. Combine the parsley with 1 tablespoon flour and spread on top of the dough. Roll into a jelly roll and cut the dough into 8 equal portions. Working with one at a time, place a portion, cut-side up on a lightly floured surface and roll into a 5 to 6-inch circle, dusting often with flour. Cover the rounds with a moist towel as you complete rolling them. Do not stack them.

3. Heat a griddle or frying pan over medium-high heat until very hot. Place a *paratha* on the griddle and let it cook for 2 to 3 minutes on each side, or until flecked with brown. Pour 2 teaspoons of oil on and around the *paratha*. Fry, turning, until it develops patches of brown on each side, about 2 minutes. Remove the bread and keep warm. Cook all the breads the same way.

4. Arrange *parathas* in a small basket and serve immediately.

MOGHUL BREAD
with Fragrant Meat Stuffing

Keema Bhara Paratha

These meat-stuffed breads, fragrant with the characteristic Moghul spices, are a popular Sunday brunch item for people in northern India. They are typically served with a cool yogurt salad, such as Banana-Coconut Yogurt Salad (page 185), an herbal chutney like Mint Chutney (page 189), and Spiced Tea (page 207). I also find these parathas delicious by themselves, particularly when cut into wedges and served with cocktails.

SERVES 6

MAKES 6 *PARATHAS*

1 recipe *chapati* (see page 44)

1 recipe Dry-cooked Spicy Ground Beef
(page 152)

3 tablespoons vegetable oil

60

1. Make the *chapati* dough through Step 1 as directed on page 44. Divide the dough into 6 equal portions. Divide the filling into 6 portions.

2. Shape 1 piece of dough into a smooth ball. Keep the remainder covered. Roll out the ball of dough on a lightly floured surface to an 8-inch circle, dusting often with flour. Spread 1 portion of filling on top. Fold the edges into the center to form a 4-inch circle, pleating and lightly pressing them to seal. Cover with a moist towel. Repeat with the remaining dough and filling. Do not stack the *parathas*.

3. Heat a griddle or frying pan over medium-high heat. Heat 1/2 teaspoon of the oil and add 1 *paratha*. Cook until it is lightly fried and spotted brown, turning a few times, about 2 minutes. Remove and keep warm Cook the other *parathas* in the same way.

4. Arrange *parathas* in a basket and serve immediately

61

SPICY POTATO-STUFFED BREAD

Aloo Paratha

With a raita *salad, this earthy and very satisfying farm-style bread with a spicy potato filling is a meal in one. For a more substantial meal serve the* parathas *with a vegetable dish.*

SERVES 6

MAKES 6 *PARATHAS*

> 1 pound potatoes, boiled, peeled, and mashed
>
> 1 teaspoon ground coriander
>
> 1/4 cup minced fresh coriander (cilantro) leaves
>   and tender stems
>
> 1/2 teaspoon ground red pepper
>
> Coarse salt to taste
>
> 1 recipe *chapati* (see page 44)
>
> 6 tablespoons vegetable oil

1. Combine the potatoes, ground coriander, fresh coriander, red pepper and salt in a bowl and mix well.

2. To prepare the *chapati* dough and make the *parathas*, follow the directions for *keema bhara paratha* on page 60, using this potato filling instead of the meat filling.

3. Arrange *parathas* on a platter and serve immediately.

TANDOORI BREAD STUFFED
with Cherries and Pistachios

Shahi Nan

A real treat for those who like bread with dried fruits and nuts. This nan is fine served on its own, but it is really wonderful with tandoori kebabs such as Chicken Ginger Kebabs (page 92) or Spice-Rubbed Grilled Lamb (page 104).

SERVES 8

MAKES 8 NANS

> 1 recipe *nan* (see page 48)
>
> ¹/₄ cup chopped dried cherries
>
> ¹/₄ cup chopped toasted pistachios

1. Prepare the *nan* dough, kneading the cherries and pistachios into the dough before dividing the dough and rolling it. Make the bread as directed on page 48.

63

SAVORY PASTRIES
with Spicy Chicken Filling

Murgh Samosa

Samosas *are classic Indian fare—little pastries with a variety of savory stuffings. They make a terrific appetizer for a special dinner party or, served with a salad, a light entree for family meals.*

SERVES 8

MAKES 12 *SAMOSAS*

SPICY CHICKEN FILLING

1 1/2 tablespoons *usli ghee* (see page 216) or clarified butter

1 teaspoon minced garlic

1 cup chopped scallions, white and green parts

1 baking potato, boiled, peeled and cubed

3/4 pound boneless and skinless chicken breast, cubed

1/2 cup peeled and finely grated carrot

2 teaspoons *Garam Masala* (page 7)

Coarse salt to taste

2 teaspoons lemon juice

SAMOSA DOUGH

1 1/2 cups all-purpose flour, plus additional flour for dusting

1/4 teaspoon nigella seeds, or 1/2 teaspoon dried oregano (optional)

1/8 teaspoon baking soda

6 tablespoons warm water

64

3 tablespoons melted *usli ghee* (see page 216)
    or clarified butter

2 tablespoons plain yogurt

1/2 teaspoon coarse salt

Cornstarch, for dusting

2 tablespoons cornstarch dissolved in
    3 tablespoons water

Peanut or corn oil, for deep-frying

1. To prepare the filling, heat a large frying pan over medium-high heat. Add the *usli ghee*, garlic, scallions, potato, chicken, and carrot. Cook, stirring occasionally, for 7 minutes, or until lightly fried. Stir in the *Garam Masala*, salt, and lemon juice. Cool. (*The filling may be prepared 1 day ahead. Cover and refrigerate. Bring to room temperature before using.*)

2. To prepare the dough, combine the flour, nigella, if using, and baking soda in a large bowl. Whisk together the water, *usli ghee*, yogurt, and salt in a measuring cup until blended. Add to the dry ingredients and stir until the dough comes together. Gather into a ball. Turn the dough out onto a floured work surface and knead until elastic, about 5 minutes. (*The dough may be prepared 1 day ahead. Wrap tightly and refrigerate. Bring to room temperature before continuing.*)

3. Line a cookie sheet with plastic wrap, dust lightly with cornstarch, and set aside. Divide the dough into 8 pieces. Shape each piece into a ball. Place 1 ball between the palms of your hands and press to flatten to a 3-inch round. Place on a floured work surface. Using a rolling pin, roll out the dough to a 6-inch round, lifting and turning frequently and dusting the work surface with flour as necessary to prevent sticking. Cut the round in half. Brush half of the straight edge of a half-round with the cornstarch mixture. Form a cone by folding the second half of the straight edge over first half and pinch the seam to seal. Hold the cone with the open end up. Stuff with 1/4 cup filling. Brush 1 side of the open end with the cornstarch mixture. Pinch the open sides together to enclose the filling. Place the *samosa* on the cookie sheet and refrigerate. Repeat with remaining dough balls, cornstarch mixture, and filling.

4. Pour the oil into a *kadhai* or a deep-fryer to a depth of 3 inches and heat to 375°. Add some *samosas* without crowding and cook until golden, turning

occasionally, about 4 minutes. Using a slotted spoon, transfer to paper towels; repeat with remaining *samosas*. (*The* samosas *may be made ahead and refrigerated for up to 2 days. To reheat, slip them into hot oil and fry for 90 seconds or spread them in a single layer on a baking sheet and place in a preheated 350° oven for 10 minutes.*)

5. Mound the *samosas* in a small, shallow basket and serve immediately.

SAVORY PASTRIES
with Spicy Vegetable Filling

Aloo Samosa

Similar to the murgh samosas *(page 64), these have a vegetable filling. Potatoes and peas, spiced with cumin, coriander, paprika, and chilies, make a flavorful stuffing. Serve these* samosas *with Mint Chutney (page 189).*

SERVES 8

MAKES 12 *SAMOSAS*

SPICY VEGETABLE FILLING

> 1 tablespoon *usli ghee* (see page 216)
>   or clarified butter
>
> 2 teaspoons cumin seeds
>
> 1 tablespoon ground coriander
>
> 1 teaspoon minced fresh chiles
>
> 2 teaspoons paprika
>
> 3 baking potatoes, boiled, peeled, and cubed
>
> 1/2 cup frozen green peas, thawed
>
> Coarse salt to taste
>
> 1/2 cup chopped fresh coriander (cilantro)
>   leaves and tender stems
>
>
> 1 recipe *Samosa* Dough (page 64)

1. Heat the *usli ghee* in a large frying pan over medium-high heat and add the cumin seeds. When the cumin gets a little darker, add the coriander, paprika, chiles, and potatoes. Cook for 5 minutes, then stir in the peas, salt, and fresh coriander leaves. Let cool. (*The filling may be prepared 1 day ahead. Cover and refrigerate. Bring to room temperature before continuing.*)

67

2. To make the *samosas*, prepare the dough, fill the half-rounds, and fry as directed in Steps 2, 3, and 4 on page 65. (*The* samosas *may be made ahead and kept refrigerated for up to 4 days. To reheat, slip them into hot oil and fry for 90 seconds or spread them out in a single layer on a baking sheet and place in a preheated 350° oven for 10 minutes.*)

3. Mound the *samosas* in a small, shallow basket and serve immediately.

68

RICE
AND GRAINS

THE Indian long grain rice called basmati, with its nutty fragrance, milky flavor, and exquisite texture, is unmatched in the world. This is the rice that is commonly used in Indian pilafs and the baked rice dish called biriyani. The rice is cooked with other ingredients such as fruits, herbs, and highly aromatic spices, such as cinnamon, cardamom, cloves, bay leaves, and cumin. The spices are usually added whole so as not to alter the glossy appearance and pure color of the rice. While cinnamon may be left as a garnish, bay leaves, cardamom pods, and cloves must be removed and discarded, even though no harm is caused by accidentally biting into one. Basmati rice is widely available, so do try to get it; there is really no good substitute. If necessary, however, you may substitute jasmine rice (another scented long-grain rice from Asia), regular long-grain rice, or converted (parboiled) rice. In addition to white rice, pilafs are made with brown basmati, cream of rice, flaked rice, semolina (Cream of Wheat is a good substitute), cracked wheat, millet, and barley.

Three Ways to Cook Perfect Basmati Rice

Each of these techniques produces perfectly cooked basmati rice.

- The first technique is the one I introduced in 1983 while I was Executive Chef at an Indian restaurant. It is similar to cooking pasta. The rice is cooked in a large quantity of boiling water then drained and served.

- The second technique is the one I learned at my mother's side in her kitchen in New Delhi; it is the classic steaming method. The rice is cooked in exactly twice the amount of water. It is first boiled, then steamed until fully cooked.

- In the third technique, known as the Moghul method, the rice is first boiled rapidly in a large quantity of water until partially cooked, then baked in the oven.

Regardless of the cooking process, basmati rice is always rinsed thoroughly and soaked in cold water for thirty minutes before cooking to permit the grains to expand better. Basmati grains are thinner than other rice grains; they have a loose inner structure and are low in starch. So soaking softens and relaxes the grains, thus reducing the amount of liquid needed and the cooking time.

Cooked basmati may be kept, covered, at room temperature for up to eight hours or refrigerated for two days. Reheat the rice in a frying pan over medium heat, stirring carefully, until heated through, or place in a preheated 350° oven, wrapped in foil, for fifteen minutes. If the rice looks dry, sprinkle a tablespoon or two of water over it before heating.

To reheat in a microwave, place rice in a microwave-safe dish, cover, and heat at 100 percent power. Four cups of cooked rice will take four minutes to reheat.

71

PERFECT BOILED BASMATI RICE

Obla Chawal

SERVES 4

1½ cups basmati rice

1. Rinse the rice thoroughly in several changes of cold water and put it in a bowl. Add enough cold water to cover the rice by 1 inch. Soak the rice for at least 30 minutes or up to 2 hours. Drain the rice.

2. While the rice is soaking, bring a large quantity of water, about 8 cups, to a boil in a deep pot. Add the drained rice and bring back to a boil, stirring occasionally with a fork to ensure that the rice does not settle at the bottom of the pan. Cook the rice for exactly 4 minutes. Remove from the heat and drain well.

3. Transfer the rice to a heated platter and serve immediately.

NOTE: If not serving immediately, drizzle 1 teaspoon *usli ghee* (see page 216) or vegetable oil over the rice, gently folding it in. Cover and set aside until ready to use.

PERFECT STEAMED BASMATI RICE

Bhapa Chawal

SERVES 4

1½ cups basmati rice

1. Rinse the rice in several changes of cold water and put it in a heavy saucepan. Add 3 cups cold water. Soak the rice for at least 30 minutes or up to 2 hours.

2. Place the saucepan with the rice and water over high heat and bring to a boil, stirring occasionally with a fork to ensure that the rice does not settle at the bottom of the pan. Reduce the heat to medium and cook the rice, partially covered, until most of the water is absorbed and the surface of the rice is covered with steam holes, about 8 minutes.

3. Cover the pan tightly and reduce the heat as low as possible. Let the rice steam for 10 minutes. Remove from the heat and let the rice rest, covered and undisturbed, for 5 minutes before serving. Fluff with a fork.

4. Transfer to a heated platter and serve immediately.

PERFECT BAKED BASMATI RICE

Dum Chawal

SERVES 4

1 ¹/₂ cups basmati rice

1 tablespoon *usli ghee* (see page 216)
or clarified butter

1. Rinse the rice in several changes of cold water and put it in a heavy saucepan. Add 3 cups cold water. Soak the rice for at least 30 minutes or up to 2 hours, then drain.

2. While the rice is soaking, preheat the oven to 325°.

3. Bring a large quantity of water, about 8 cups, to a boil in a deep pot. Add the drained rice and bring back to a boil. Stir occasionally with a fork to ensure that the rice does not settle at the bottom of the pan. Cook for exactly 2 ¹/₂ minutes. Drain the rice and put it in an ovenproof casserole with a lid. Add the *usli ghee*, mix carefully, cover and bake in the middle level of the oven for 25 minutes. Turn off the oven and let the rice rest, covered and undisturbed, for 10 minutes. Fluff with a fork.

4. Transfer to a heated platter and serve.

LEMON PILAF

Chitrannam

A subtly flavored and visually appealing lemon rice from South India brings forth the very essence of Indian summer. It is a good pilaf to serve with steamed and grilled fish and shellfish such as Steamed Fish in Herb Sauce (page 112) or Parsi Breaded Shrimp in Green Paste (page 124).

SERVES 4

1 tablespoon vegetable oil

1 teaspoon mustard seeds

$1/4$ teaspoon asafetida, or $1/2$ teaspoon minced garlic

$1/2$ teaspoon turmeric

$1 1/2$ tablespoons lemon juice

$2 1/2$ cups cooked rice made with 1 cup raw rice (basmati, brown rice, or converted rice)

$1/4$ cup chopped roasted cashews

Coarse salt to taste

$1/2$ teaspoon minced green chiles (optional)

12 kari leaves, fresh or dried (optional)

1 firm, ripe mango, peeled, pitted, and diced into $1/2$-inch pieces, for garnish (optional)

1. Heat the oil in a heavy saucepan over medium-high heat. When the oil is hot, add the mustard seeds and cover the pan with the lid because the seeds will pop and spatter. When the spluttering subsides, add the asafetida, turmeric, lemon juice, and 3 tablespoons water and bring to a boil.

2. Stir in the rice, cashews, and salt, and the chiles and kari leaves, if using. Toss well until the rice is evenly seasoned.

3. Serve hot, at room temperature, or cold, garnished with mango, if desired.

PEACH AND WALNUT BASMATI PILAF

Khoobani Pulao

Fruit pilaf is a classic Moghul creation and this peach pilaf is one of the best. The combination of fruit and nuts with the fragrant rice provides a truly sensuous experience. It is perfect with Tandoori Chicken (page 90) or Malabar Coconut Shrimp (page 122).

SERVES 6

> 1 1/2 cups basmati or regular long-grain rice
>
> 3 cups peaches, peeled and sliced
>
> 1/2 teaspoon ground ginger
>
> 1/2 teaspoon ground fennel
>
> 1/4 teaspoon grated nutmeg
>
> 2 tablespoons *usli ghee* (see page 216)
>   or clarified butter
>
> 1/3 cup walnut pieces

1. Rinse the rice in several changes of cold water and put in a bowl. Add enough cold water to cover the rice by 1 inch. Soak the rice for at least 30 minutes or up to 2 hours. Drain.

2. Combine 1 cup of the peach slices and 1 cup water in a food processor and process until the fruit is liquefied. Add enough water to make 3 cups peach juice. Stir in the ginger, fennel, and nutmeg.

3. Transfer the spiced peach juice to a heavy saucepan. Add the rice and bring to a boil, stirring occasionally with a fork to ensure that the rice does not settle at the bottom of the pan. Reduce the heat to medium and cook, partially covered, for 8 minutes for basmati rice (13 minutes for regular rice), or until most of the water is absorbed and the surface of the rice is covered with several steam holes. Cover the pan tightly and reduce the heat as low as possible. Let the rice steam for 10 minutes. Remove from the heat and let the rice rest, covered and undisturbed, for 5 minutes.

4. Heat the *usli ghee* in a frying pan and add the walnuts. Fry the nuts, shaking and stirring, for 1 minute. Add the remaining peaches and cook until the fruit is warmed through and glazed, about 2 minutes. Fluff the rice with a fork.

5. Transfer to a heated platter. Scatter peach slices and walnuts on top and serve immediately.

ORANGE-CINNAMON BASMATI PILAF

Naarangi Pulao

This is a highly aromatic citrus-sweet pilaf that showcases the beautiful flavor of the basmati rice. Because of its keeping quality, orange-cinnamon pilaf is perfect for picnics or for buffet tables. This pilaf is totally salt and fat-free. Serve the pilaf with Country Captain (page 136) or Malabar Coconut Shrimp (page 122).

SERVES 4

1 cup raw brown basmati or regular brown rice

3/4 cup orange juice

1 stick (3 inches) cinnamon

5 whole cloves

1/2 teaspoon grated fresh ginger

1/4 cup dark raisins

Orange slices, for garnish (optional)

1. Rinse the rice well with cold water and place in a bowl. Add 1 1/2 cups cold water and let soak for at least 30 minutes or up to 2 hours. Drain the rice, reserving the water.

2. Meanwhile, place a saucepan over high heat. Add all the other ingredients, including the reserved water, except the orange slices and bring to a boil. Reduce the heat to medium. Drain the rice and add to the saucepan. Cook, partially covered, for 15 minutes for basmati rice (18 minutes for regular rice), or until most of the moisture is absorbed and the surface of the rice is covered with steam holes. Cover the pan tightly and reduce the heat as low as possible.

3. Let the rice steam for 10 minutes. Remove from the heat and let the rice rest, covered, for 5 minutes. Remove the cinnamon stick and cloves and fluff with a fork.

4. Transfer to a heated platter, garnish with orange slices, if desired, and serve.

79

GREEN PEA PILAF

Matar Pulao

This pearl-white pilaf, studded with forest green peas, is a Moghul classic. Because of its subtle, mellow flavor, it is the most popular rice pilaf at Indian restaurants. The pilaf can be cooked either in a rich chicken stock or plain water. It is wonderful both ways.

SERVES 4

1 1/2 cups basmati or regular long-grain rice

2 tablespoons vegetable oil

1/2 teaspoon cumin seeds

4 green whole cardamom pods

2 whole cloves

1 bay leaf

1/2 cup chopped onion

1/2 teaspoon ground ginger

3 cups Chicken Stock (page 36) or water

Coarse salt to taste

1 package frozen green peas (10 ounces),
    thawed

1. Rinse the rice well with cold water and put it in a bowl. Add cold water to cover the rice by 1 inch and soak for at least 30 minutes or up to 2 hours. Drain.

2. Heat the oil in a saucepan over medium-high heat. When the oil is hot, add the cumin, cardamom, cloves, and bay leaf. When the cumin turns several shades darker, add the onion. Cook until the onion begins to brown, about 5 minutes. Add the rice, ginger, stock, and salt to taste and bring to a boil. Lower the heat and cook, partially covered, for 8 minutes for basmati rice (12 minutes for regular rice), or until most of the liquid is absorbed and the surface of the rice is covered with steam holes. Cover the pan, and reduce the heat to low.

3. Let the rice steam for 10 minutes. Remove from the heat, stir in the peas, and let the rice rest, covered, for 5 minutes. Remove the cardamom, cloves, and bay leaf and fluff the rice with a fork.

4. Transfer to a heated platter and serve.

81

CURRIED RICE

Masala Bhat

This dish is the specialty of the Tamil Christians of South India. It is similar to the pilafs of North India but much simpler. I frequently make this rice dish to accompany simple sautéed or grilled chicken or seafood such as Pan-grilled Scallops with Ajowan (page 120).

SERVES 4

1/4 cup finely chopped onion

1 teaspoon minced garlic

1 tablespoon vegetable oil

1 cup converted rice

1 1/2 teaspoons Curry Powder (page 6)

2 cups Chicken Stock (page 36) or water

2 tablespoons finely chopped fresh coriander
   (cilantro) leaves

1 teaspoon coarse salt or to taste

1. Heat a heavy saucepan over medium-high heat. Add the onion, garlic, and oil and cook until the onion looks soft, about 2 minutes. Mix in the rice, Curry Powder, stock, fresh coriander, and salt. Bring to a boil. Reduce the heat and cook, covered, for 20 minutes or until the rice is cooked and the liquid is absorbed. Fluff the rice with a fork

2. Transfer to a heated platter and serve.

MINT RICE

Podina Chawal

A Persian and Moghul classic, this pilaf has many interpretations throughout India. This version is from the Himachal community at the extreme north, in the foothills of the Himalayas. Serve it with a curry such as Lamb Curry *(page 144) or* Chicken Curry *(page 130).*

SERVES 4

> ¹/₄ cup finely chopped shallot
>
> 2 tablespoons minced mint
>
> 1 tablespoon vegetable oil
>
> 1 cup converted rice
>
> 2 cups Chicken Stock (page 36) or water
>
> 1 teaspoon coarse salt or to taste
>
> 2 tablespoons toasted pine nuts, for garnish

1. Heat a heavy saucepan over medium-high heat. Add the shallot, mint, and oil. Cook until the shallot is lightly fried, about 3 minutes. Add the rice, stock, and salt and bring to a boil. Reduce the heat and cook, covered, for 20 minutes, or until the rice is cooked and the liquid is absorbed. Fluff the rice with a fork.

2. Transfer to a heated platter. Garnish with the pine nuts and serve.

83

SAFFRON PILAF

Zaffran Pulao

Delicately flavored with the spices saffron and clove and embellished with raisins and nuts, this pilaf is perfect with the royal dishes of the Moghul.

SERVES 6

1/2 teaspoon saffron threads

1 cup basmati or regular long-grain rice

1 tablespoon *usli ghee* (see page 216)
    or vegetable oil

1/2 cup chopped onion

2 tablespoons dark raisins

3 whole cloves

1 3/4 cups Chicken Stock (page 36)

Coarse salt

2 tablespoons toasted sliced almonds

84

1. Crumble $1/4$ teaspoon of the saffron threads with your fingertips and put in a small bowl. Add the remaining saffron and 1 tablespoon warm water and set aside to soak. Rinse the basmati thoroughly with cold water and put it in a large bowl. Add 2 cups cold water and soak for at least 30 minutes or up to 2 hours. Drain the rice and set aside. Discard the water.

2. Heat the *usli ghee* in a saucepan over medium-high heat. Add the onion, raisins, and cloves. Cook, stirring constantly, until the onions look glazed, about 5 minutes. Add the stock, saffron solution, rice, and salt to taste. Bring to a boil.

3. Reduce the heat to medium and cook the rice, partially covered, for 8 minutes for basmati rice (13 minutes for regular rice) or until most of the liquid is absorbed and the surface of the rice is covered with steam holes. Cover the pan tightly and reduce the heat to as low as possible. Let the rice steam for 10 minutes. Remove from the heat and let the rice rest, covered and undisturbed, for 5 minutes. Fluff the rice with a fork.

4. Transfer to a heated platter, sprinkle the almonds on top, and serve.

85

SEMOLINA PILAF

Opama

In this popular pilaf from South India, the heat can range from very mild to fiery hot! I use very mild chiles, such as Anaheim, to keep the heat level low so that the subtle flavor of the semolina is not masked. For more flavor, add 12 kari leaves with the shallots. Opama is best with spicy dishes such as Cornish Hen Vindaloo (see page 138) or Malabar Coconut Shrimp (page 122).

SERVES 6

¹/₄ cup vegetable oil

1 cup semolina or Cream of Wheat

1¹/₂ teaspoons mustard seeds

³/₄ cup chopped shallots

1 tablespoon chopped green chiles

1 tablespoon chopped fresh ginger

1 cup yogurt

Coarse salt to taste

¹/₄ cup chopped roasted cashews (optional)

1. Heat 2 tablespoons of the oil in a large heavy sauté pan. Add the semolina and fry until the grains are evenly coated with the oil and lightly colored, about 6 minutes. Transfer to a bowl and wipe the pan clean with a paper towel.

2. Pour the remaining 2 tablespoons of oil into the pan. When it is hot, add the mustard seeds and cover the pan with the lid because the seeds will pop and spatter. When the spluttering subsides, add the shallots, chiles, and ginger and mix well. Whisk together the yogurt and $1\,^1/_4$ cups water and add to the pan. Add the semolina and salt. Cook, stirring gently, until the mixture thickens, about 5 minutes.

3. Reduce the heat, cover, and cook for 5 minutes, or until most of the liquid is absorbed and the pilaf looks like dry polenta. Remove from the heat and let the pilaf rest, covered, for 10 minutes to become drier and fluffier. Fluff the pilaf with a fork. Transfer to a heated serving platter, sprinkle with the cashews, if using, and serve.

NOTE: To make the pilaf more substantial, add $^1/_2$ cup chopped green or red bell pepper, $^1/_2$ cup diced eggplant, and $^1/_2$ cup sliced mushrooms with the shallot. Check and adjust the amount of salt before serving.

87

TANDOORI GRILLING

IN Indian baking, roasting, and grilling are done in a *tandoor,* a clay oven that is thought to have originated in Syria but today is used throughout central Asia. The Indians initially used the oven to bake bread, and this is still its main use. The breads, called *nan* (see page 48) are slapped onto the sides of the *tandoor;* it sticks on, puffs up, and bakes. Any meat, poultry, fish, or vegetable that can be threaded on skewers can also be cooked in a *tandoor.* The skewers are lowered into the *tandoor* pit and cooked. The meat remains tender and moist because it has been marinated in yogurt flavored with herbs and spices. Instructions in this chapter are for cooking *tandoor*-style dishes in a conventional oven or on a grill. I have created special marinades to replace the unique flavor of the *tandoor.*

TANDOORI CHICKEN	90
TANDOORI MURGH	
CHICKEN GINGER KEBABS	92
MURGH TIKKA	
TANDOORI FISH	94
TANDOORI MACHI	
TANDOORI SHRIMP	96
TANDOORI JHEENGA	
MOGHUL BEEF KEBAB	98
PASANDA KABAB	
INDIAN-STYLE HAMBURGER	100
CHAPLI KABAB	
MOGHUL LAMB KEBABS	102
BOTI KABAB	
SPICE-RUBBED GRILLED LAMB	104
BHONA GOSHT	
TANDOORI VEGETABLES	106
TANDOORI SABZI	

TANDOORI CHICKEN

Tandoori Murgh

For Tandoori Chicken, the meat is marinated in yogurt spiced with ginger, garlic, and other fragrant spices and then cooked in a tandoor, where it roasts and grills simultaneously. In order for the marinade to permeate the meat, the chicken is skinned and the meat pricked and slashed.

SERVES 4

2 small chickens (about 2 1/4 pounds each),
    split or quartered

2 tablespoons lemon juice

2 tablespoons yellow food coloring (optional)

1 tablespoon red food coloring (optional)

2 tablespoons ground cumin

1 tablespoon *Garam Masala* (page 7)
    or ground coriander

1 to 2 teaspoons ground red pepper

Coarse salt to taste

2 cups yogurt

2 tablespoons grated fresh ginger

1 tablespoon minced garlic

6 tablespoons *usli ghee* (see page 216),
    clarified butter or extra-virgin olive oil

Onion, tomato, and cucumber slices,
    for garnish

1. Pull the skin off the chicken pieces, remove all visible fat, and discard. Prick the chicken all over with a fork and make diagonal slashes, $1/2$ inch deep and 1 inch apart, on the meat. Mix together the lemon juice, food colorings, if using, cumin, *Garam Masala*, red pepper, and salt and brush over the chicken, pushing the marinade into the slits. Combine the yogurt, ginger, and garlic and pour over the chicken. Mix, turning several times, to coat the chicken pieces evenly with the marinade. Cover and marinate at room temperature for 1 hour or refrigerate for 8 hours or up to 2 days.

2. If the chicken has been refrigerated, bring to room temperature before cooking. If grilling, heat the grill and place the grill rack at least 5 inches from the heat. If roasting, place the oven rack in the middle position and preheat the oven to 500°.

3. Remove the chicken from the marinade and coat generously with *usli ghee*. To grill, place meat side down, on the grill rack. To roast, place the chicken, meat side down, on a wire rack set over a jelly-roll pan. Grill or roast the chicken, turning 3 or 4 times during cooking, until the juices run clear, about 35 minutes. Brush the chicken with the remaining *usli ghee* and transfer to a platter.

4. Surround the chicken with slices of onion, tomato, and cucumber and serve.

NOTE: The tandoori marinade is traditionally colored bright orange using natural food coloring. This is purely for visual effect. You can omit the color if you prefer.

CHICKEN GINGER KEBABS

Murgh Tikka

Chicken kebabs are similar to Tandoori Chicken except that boneless chicken meat is used. Cut into bite-size pieces, the kebabs can be served as finger-food at a cocktail reception; pass them with Mint Chutney (page 189). For a more elaborate meal, serve them with a Peach and Walnut Basmati Pilaf (page 76) or Baked Tandoori Bread (page 48) and Indian Salsa (page 196).

SERVES 4

2 pounds skinless and boneless chicken meat,
cut into 1 1/2 inch pieces

MARINADE

1 cup sour cream

3 tablespoons white wine vinegar

2 tablespoons grated fresh ginger

1 teaspoon minced garlic

1 tablespoon finely chopped green chiles

1/2 teaspoon crushed ajowan seeds,
or 1 teaspoon thyme

1 tablespoon ground coriander

Coarse salt to taste

4 tablespoons olive oil, for basting

GARNISH

Green and red bell pepper slices

Thinly sliced scallions, white and green parts

Fresh coriander (cilantro) leaves and tender
stems

Lemon wedges

1. Put the chicken pieces in a large ceramic or glass bowl. Blend together all the marinade ingredients in another bowl. Pour the marinade over the chicken. Stir well to coat all the chicken pieces thoroughly. Cover and marinate at room temperature for 1 hour or refrigerate for 4 hours or up to 1 day.

2. If the chicken has been refrigerated, bring to room temperature before cooking. If grilling, heat the grill and place the grill rack at least 5 inches from the heat. To roast, preheat the oven to 500°.

3. Thread the chicken pieces on skewers. To grill, brush the skewers with oil and grill, turning often, until fully cooked, about 7 minutes. To roast, brush the skewers with oil and place in a single layer on a wire rack set over a jelly-roll pan. Roast, turning and basting with oil until the kebabs are fully cooked, about 10 minutes. Do not overcook, as they dry out easily.

4. Slide the kebabs off the skewers and arrange them on a heated platter. Surround them with pepper slices, scallions, coriander, and lemon wedges, and serve.

93

TANDOORI FISH

Tandoori Machi

Tandoori Fish is the specialty of the Bengali Catholics of Portuguese descent. Although not as well known as Goan Portuguese food, Bengali Portuguese food, particularly certain fish preparations, is distinct and noteworthy. In this dish, fish kebabs, delicately flavored with a special tandoori marinade are cooked to perfection. Serve the kebabs with any rice dish and, if you wish, a vegetable, such as Green Beans in Fenugreek Oil (page 160).

SERVES 4

1 ½ pounds skinless and boneless, firm white
fish, such as sea bass, turbot, or monkfish,
cut into 1 ½-inch cubes

MARINADE

1 teaspoon minced garlic

2 teaspoons grated fresh ginger

2 tablespoons heavy cream

1 tablespoon yellow food coloring (optional)

½ teaspoon ajowan seeds, crushed,
or 1 teaspoon thyme

½ teaspoon freshly ground black pepper

Coarse salt to taste

2 onions, peeled and cut into 1-inch pieces

2 green peppers, cored and cut into 1-inch
pieces

2 tablespoons melted butter for basting

GARNISH

> 3 lemons, sliced
>
> 3 tomatoes, sliced
>
> 2 tablespoons chopped fresh coriander
> (cilantro) leaves

1. Put the fish pieces in a large ceramic or glass bowl. Add all the marinade ingredients and toss well. Cover and marinate the fish for 30 minutes or refrigerate for 4 hours or up to 8 hours.

2. Preheat the grill or broiler. Place the grill rack 5 inches from the heat.

3. Thread the fish pieces on skewers alternating with pieces of onion and pepper. Brush generously with butter and place them in a single layer on the grill or under the broiler. Grill or broil, turning once and basting, until the fish is barely opaque, 5 to 6 minutes.

4. Transfer the fish to a heated platter. Garnish with the lemon and tomato slices and chopped coriander and serve.

95

TANDOORI SHRIMP

Tandoori Jheenga

These grilled shrimps are great for large-scale entertaining. Besides being attractive and delicious, they are very quick to make. For a light meal serve a salad with them. For a more elaborate meal include a pilaf, such as Saffron Pilaf (page 84), and Cauliflower with Nigella in Ginger Oil (page 164).

SERVES 4

1 1/2 pounds large shrimp, peeled and deveined with tails left on

MARINADE

3 tablespoons yogurt

2 teaspoons grated fresh or prepared horseradish

1 tablespoon yellow food coloring (optional)

1 tablespoon minced garlic

1 tablespoon grated fresh ginger

2 teaspoons dry mustard

1/2 teaspoon ground red pepper

Coarse salt to taste

2 onions, peeled and cut into 1-inch pieces

2 red bell peppers, cored and cut into 1-inch pieces

2 tablespoons melted butter for basting

GARNISH

Tomato, cucumber, and lemon slices

1. Put the shrimp in a large ceramic bowl or glass bowl. Add all of the marinade ingredients and toss well. Cover and marinate the shrimp for at least 10 minutes, or up to 30 minutes.

2. Preheat the grill or broiler. Place the grill rack 5 inches from the heat.

3. Thread the shrimp on skewers, alternating with pieces of onion and pepper. Brush generously with butter and place them in a single layer on the grill rack or under the broiler. Grill or broil, turning often and basting, until the shrimp curl and turn pink, 6 to 7 minutes.

4. Transfer the skewers to a heated platter. Garnish with the tomato, cucumber, and lemon slices and serve.

97

MOGHUL BEEF KEBABS

Pasanda Kabab

Pasanda *means delicious pieces and that is what these succulent morsels of spicy beef are. Yet another Moghul classic, they are the specialty of Pakistan, the country with which India shares the rich Moghul heritage. These kebabs are similar to Moghul Lamb Kebabs (page 102) except that here the marinade is accented with cardamom. A simple green salad and plain cooked rice will complete the meal.*

SERVES 4

1 1/2 pounds beef sirloin, trimmed of excess fat,
and cubed into 1 1/2-inch pieces

MARINADE

1 cup plain yogurt

1/4 cup lemon juice

2 teaspoons minced garlic

2 teaspoons grated fresh ginger

2 teaspoons ground cumin

2 teaspoons dry mustard

1 teaspoon ground cardamom

3 tablespoons melted butter or extra virgin
olive oil, for basting

Coarse salt and black pepper

GARNISH

1 small head lettuce, cored and shredded

12 red radishes

1. Pound the beef pieces, one at a time, to flatten them slightly. Set aside.

2. Combine all the marinade ingredients in a large bowl. Add the beef and mix, turning the meat several times to coat well with the marinade. Cover and marinate at room temperature for 1 hour or refrigerate overnight or for up to 2 days.

3. If the beef has been refrigerated, bring to room temperature before cooking. To grill, preheat the grill and place the grill rack at least 5 inches from the heat. To roast, preheat the oven to 475°.

4. Lift the meat from the marinade and thread on skewers. Brush liberally with melted butter. To grill, place the skewers on the grill rack and cook, turning and basting frequently, until cooked, about 10 minutes. To roast, arrange the skewers in a single layer on a wire rack set over a jelly-rollpan. Roast, turning and basting frequently, until cooked, about 8 minutes. The meat should be crusty on the outside and still pink in the middle.

5. To serve, slide the kebabs off the skewers onto a heated platter and sprinkle with salt and pepper. Surround the kebabs with lettuce and radishes. Serve immediately.

INDIAN-STYLE HAMBURGERS

Chapli Kabab

These kebabs, though shaped and cooked like American hamburgers, are, in fact, a Moghul classic. They can be made with ground lamb, beef, veal, chicken, or pork. Serve them in Indian bread or in hamburger rolls or pita pockets, if you like, topped with lettuce, onion, and tomato slices. The patties may be fried or grilled.

SERVES 4

1 pound ground lamb or beef

1 tablespoon *usli ghee* (see page 216)
    or unsalted butter, melted

1 tablespoon thinly sliced green chiles

1/2 cup (lightly packed) chopped fresh coriander
    (cilantro) leaves and tender stems

1 cup finely chopped onion

1 teaspoon *Garam Masala* (page 7)

1/2 teaspoon black pepper

Coarse salt to taste

Usli ghee, for brushing the grill

1. Combine all the ingredients thoroughly and shape into 4 hamburger patties.

2. To fry, heat a well-seasoned heavy griddle over medium-high heat. Add the patties. Cook, turning once, to the desired doneness, about 2 minutes on each side for rare, 3 minutes for medium, and 4 minutes for well done. To grill the hamburgers, heat the grill, arrange the grill rack 2 inches away from the heat, and brush lightly with *usli ghee*. Place the meat on the rack and grill, turning once, until done. The timing is the same as for frying.

Moghul Lamb Kebabs

Boti Kabab

Similar to shish kebab, these lamb kebabs are marinated in spiced yogurt flavored with plenty of cumin and black pepper and grilled to a melting tenderness. For a more complex flavoring add one tablespoon Garam Masala (page 7) to the marinade. Beef, pork, venison, and—a recent craze—buffalo all work well in this recipe. All the rice pilafs and breads in this book go well with these kebabs.

SERVES 4

1 1/2 pounds lean boneless leg of lamb, trimmed
of excess fat, and cut into 1 1/2-inch cubes

MARINADE

1 cup plain yogurt

1/4 cup red wine vinegar

1 tablespoon minced garlic

2 teaspoons grated fresh ginger

2 tablespoons ground cumin

2 to 3 teaspoons cracked black peppercorns,
preferably Tellicherry

1 teaspoon ground red pepper

Coarse salt to taste

3 tablespoons *usli ghee* (see page 216), clarified
butter, or vegetable oil, for basting

GARNISH

1/2 head lettuce, chopped

Green pepper slices

Carrot slices

1. Pound the lamb pieces, one at a time, to flatten them slightly. Set aside.

2. Combine all the marinade ingredients in a large bowl. Add the lamb and. mix, turning the meat several times to coat well with the marinade. Cover and marinate at room temperature for 1 hour or refrigerate overnight or for up to 2 days.

3. If the lamb has been refrigerated, bring to room temperatue before cooking. Heat the grill and place the grill rack at least 5 inches from the heat. To roast, preheat the oven to 475°. Lift the meat from the marinade and thread on skewers. Brush liberally with *usli ghee*.

3. To grill, place the skewers on the grill rack and cook, turning and basting frequently, until cooked, about 10 minutes. To roast, arrange the skewers in a single layer on a wire rack set over a jelly-roll pan. Roast, turning and basting, until cooked, about 8 minutes. The meat should be crusty on the outside and still pink in the middle.

4. To serve, slide the kebabs off the skewers onto a heated platter and garnish with the lettuce, pepper, and carrot.

Spice-rubbed Grilled Lamb

Bhona Gosht

An Anglo-Indian specialty, Bhona Gosht is a true Raj period classic. It is popular in many of the exclusive Raj-style clubs in India, where the dish is still called Roast Mutton. A leg of lamb is boned and butterflied for ease of serving, then rubbed with seasonings. The meat can be left flat and grilled, or rolled and tied and roasted. Sweet fruit chutneys and Mint Rice (page 83) make ideal accompaniments. Any leftover meat can be sliced and served plain in a sandwich or stir-fried with vegetables, as in Country Captain (page 136) or Beef Frazer (page 156).

SERVES 8

4 pounds boneless leg of lamb

SPICE RUB

1 tablespoon cumin seeds, crushed

1 tablespoon mustard seeds, crushed

1 tablespoon cracked black peppercorns

2 tablespoons paprika

2 tablespoons minced mint

2 tablespoons finely chopped garlic

1/3 cup white wine or lemon juice

1/4 cup *usli ghee* or clarified butter, for basting

Coarse salt and black pepper

GARNISH

1 pound red, black, or white grapes

Mint sprigs

1. Score the thickest parts of the meat and pound to an even thickness. Prick the meat all over with a fork. Transfer to a shallow roasting pan. Combine all the spice rub ingredients and rub over the meat. Cover and marinate at room temperature for 2 hours or refrigerate overnight or for up to 3 days.

2. Heat the grill and arrange the grill rack 5 inches from the heat.

3. Brush the meat liberally with 2 tablespoons of the *usli ghee*. Place the meat on the rack and grill, turning once and basting, until cooked according to taste: about 8 minutes per side for medium-rare, 9 minutes for medium, and 10 minutes for well done. Let the meat rest on a carving board for 5 minutes before slicing.

4. Sprinkle the meat with salt and pepper, slice across the grain into thin slices, and arrange on a warm platter. Brush with the remaining *usli ghee* and surround with small bunches of grapes and mint sprigs. Serve immediately.

TANDOORI VEGETABLES

Tandoori Sabzi

To satisfy the vegetarian's desire for a tandoori-style dish, vegetables are coated with a yogurt marinade and grilled. The food coloring, though traditional, may be omitted if desired; the flavor will be the same. Serve the skewers with Tandoori Bread Stuffed with Cherries and Pistachios (page 63).

SERVES 4

8 cups vegetables cut into 2-inch pieces
(see Note)

MARINADE

2 cups yogurt

$^1/_4$ cup red wine vinegar

6 tablespoons vegetable oil

3 tablespoons grated fresh ginger

1 tablespoon minced garlic

2 tablespoons yellow food coloring (optional)

1 tablespoon red food coloring (optional)

3 tablespoons ground cumin

1 tablespoon *Garam Masala* (page 7)

1 to 2 teaspoons ground red pepper

Coarse salt to taste

$^1/_3$ cup *usli ghee* (see page 216), clarified
butter, or vegetable oil, for basting

GARNISH

Lemon slices and coriander sprigs

1. Put the vegetables in a large bowl. Combine all the marinade ingredients and pour over the vegetables. Toss well to coat each piece with the marinade. Cover and marinate at room temperature for 4 hours or refrigerate for up to 2 days.

2. If the vegetables have been refrigerated, bring to room temperature before cooking. To grill, heat the grill and place the grill rack at least 3 inches from the heat. To roast, place the oven rack in the middle position and preheat the oven to 500°.

3. Remove the vegetables from the marinade and thread them on skewers. Coat generously with 3 tablespoons *usli ghee*, place on the rack, and grill, turning and basting several times, until cooked and browned, about 25 minutes. Brush the vegetables with the remaining *usli ghee* and transfer to a platter.

4. Surround the vegetables with lemon slices and coriander sprigs and serve.

NOTE: Use a combination of at least 4 vegetables, such as cauliflower, red bell pepper, green bell pepper, turnip, mushrooms, zucchini, yellow squash, pattypan squash, brussels sprouts, endive, radish, eggplant, onion, shallots, and/or scallions.

107

FISH
AND SHELLFISH

SURROUNDED on three sides by ocean, India has a rich tradition of cooking fish and shellfish. Tuna, sea bass, trout, sole, salmon, and kingfish are common everyday fare, while lobsters, shrimps, giant prawns, tiny mussels, and squid are treated with great creativity. The four distinct communities excelling in this art are the Bengalis in the east, the Tamils in the south, and the Malabaris and Goans to the southwest. Bengalis are famous for their mustard-laced fish, the Tamils for their tamarind-flavored fish, and the Malabaris and Goans for their use of coconut and chiles. The recipes chosen for this book are made with the most readily available fish and shellfish in the market, which adapt perfectly to Indian cooking. Remember your dish is going to be only as good as the ingredients, so buy only the freshest avaialble. It is quite acceptable to use substitutes, and I have made recommendations to guide you.

SMOKED SALMON KEDGEREE
with Dill

Kedgeree

Kedgeree is the Anglicized pronunciation of the Indian kecheree, a popular North Indian rice and lentil dish that looks much like risotto. The English replaced the lentils with cooked or smoked fish, added herbs and cream sauce, and turned peasant fare into an elegant brunchtime delicacy. Kedgeree is very popular with Anglo-Indians, who make it with locally available seafood, including smoked trout, sardines, sole, sea bass, Bombay duck (a type of flying fish), shrimp, mussels, and scallops. While salmon is not an Indian fish, I think it works well here, both in taste and visual appeal. You can use any smoked fish in place of the salmon.

SERVES 4

4 ounces smoked salmon, cut into bite-size
    pieces

$1/2$ teaspoon coarsely ground black pepper

2 tablespoons chopped dill

3 tablespoons unsalted butter

1 teaspoon coarse salt or to taste

1 cup converted rice

$1/4$ cup finely diced onion

1 tablespoon all-purpose flour

$1^1/4$ cups milk

6 hard-boiled eggs, peeled and cut into wedges
    (optional)

1 lemon, cut into wedges (optional)

2 tablespoons chopped parsley

Dill sprigs for garnish

1. Toss the salmon with pepper and 1 tablespoon dill and set aside.

2. Combine 2 cups water, 1 tablespoon of the butter, and salt in a medium saucepan. Bring to a boil over high heat. Stir in the rice, reduce the heat to medium-low, and simmer, covered, for 20 minutes, or until the water is absorbed and the rice is tender.

3. Melt the remaining 2 tablespoons butter in a large frying pan over medium-high heat. Add the onion and cook until soft, about 3 minutes. Add the flour and cook, stirring, until it is fried but not browned, about 2 minutes. Add the milk and the remaining dill and cook, stirring constantly, for 2 minutes or until the sauce thickens. Reduce the heat, fold in the rice and cook until heated through. Transfer to a heated serving platter.

4. Arrange the salmon on top of the rice and surround with the egg and lemon wedges, if using. Sprinkle with parsley, garnish with dill, and serve.

III

STEAMED FISH
in Herb Sauce

Patrani Machi

Bombay's Parsi community excels in fish cookery, and Patrani Machi *is their signature dish. (The Parsis are a sect that was driven out of Persia in the ninth century and settled in India's western coastal region.) Traditionally, this dish is made with hilsa, a local fish known for both its rich flavor and its innumerable bones, and is steamed in banana leaves. I have found that salmon fillets make a flavorful, appealing, and convenient substitute. I also prefer to use edible wrappers, such as lettuce (you can also use spinach, swiss chard, cabbage, and taro leaves). This dish is traditionally served with steamed rice, but is also good with a light pilaf, such as Lemon Pilaf (page 75). It can be made ahead and served straight from the refrigerator as a first course.*

SERVES 4

1¹/₂ pounds boneless and skinless salmon
    fillets

HERB SAUCE

¹/₃ cup sweetened shredded coconut

3 garlic cloves, peeled

1 to 4 green chiles, stemmed (depending on
    desired level of heat)

3 tablespoons lemon juice

¹/₂ cup (highly packed) fresh coriander
    (cilantro) leaves and tender stems

¹/₄ cup (highly packed) mint leaves

Coarse salt to taste

8 large lettuce leaves, blanched and trimmed

GARNISH

> 2 tablespoons finely chopped toasted almonds
>
> 1 teaspoon toasted cumin seeds
>
> 1 tablespoon finely chopped fresh ginger
>
> 1 teaspoon finely minced lemon zest

1. Cut the fish into 4 serving portions and set aside.

2. Rinse the coconut under warm running water and drain. Combine the coconut, garlic, chiles, lemon juice, fresh coriander, and mint in the workbowl of a food processor and process until minced. Transfer to a bowl. Stir in the salt. Add the fish and toss well to coat.

3. Place 2 lettuce leaves on a work surface, overlapping them slightly. Place 1 piece of fish on top of the lettuce leaves, fold in the sides, and close up into a neat package. Prepare the remaining pieces the same way. Transfer the packages to a steamer rack or put 2 packages in each of 2 bamboo steamer trays. Steam until the fish is just cooked, about 6 minutes.

4. To serve, transfer the fish packets to warm dinner plates and open leaves.

113

BENGAL FRAGRANT FISH CURRY

Maach Bhaja

An everyday dish from Bengal in eastern India, this is a light fish dish with lots of spices in a tomato sauce. Plain rice is the best choice to serve with it.

SERVES 4

4 cod, haddock, or tuna steaks

1 teaspoon dry mustard

1 teaspoon ground cumin

$1/2$ teaspoon turmeric

$1/2$ teaspoon ground red pepper

2 tablespoons mustard oil (see page 214)
   or vegetable oil

1 cup thinly sliced onion

1 tablespoon sliced garlic

1 tablespoon shredded green chiles

2 cups chopped peeled tomatoes

Coarse salt to taste

Juice of $1/2$ lemon

$1/4$ cup finely chopped fresh coriander (cilantro)
   leaves and tender stems

1. Place the fish steaks on a plate and sprinkle with mustard, cumin, turmeric, and red pepper. Rub the spices all over the fish and set aside. Heat 1 tablespoon of the oil in a large heavy nonstick sauté pan over high heat. If you are using the mustard oil, let it smoke for a moment to rid it of its pungency. Add the fish and sauté, turning once, until seared, about 1 minute. Transfer to a plate.

2. Reduce the heat to medium and add the remaining oil, the onion, garlic, and chiles. Cook, stirring occasionally, until the onion begins to brown, about 5 minutes. Add 1 cup of the tomatoes, along with the accumulated juices, and salt. Continue to cook until the sauce thickens a little, about 5 minutes. Add the fish steaks and the remaining tomatoes and cook until the sauce is bubbling and the fish is heated through, about 4 minutes. Transfer the fish and the sauce to a heated serving platter.

3. Sprinkle with lemon juice and fresh coriander and serve.

MADRAS HOT FISH CURRY
with Tamarind

Meen Kari

Try this dish even if you have never cooked with tamarind before. In this specialty from Tamil Nadu on the southern shores of India, the fish gets its piquant flavor from the tamarind and heat from red pepper. Traditionally meen kari is made very hot, but you can tone down the heat by reducing the amount of red pepper. Remember, however, to reduce the tamarind, too, or the dish will taste too sour. Serve with plain rice and Banana-Coconut Yogurt Salad (page 185).

SERVES 4

1 1/2 pounds skinless and boneless sole
   or flounder fillets, cut into 4 serving pieces

1 tablespoon curry powder

1 tablespoon ground red pepper, paprika,
   or a combination

3 tablespoons vegetable oil

1/4 cup all-purpose flour for dusting

1 teaspoon mustard seeds

1/2 cup finely chopped onion

1 teaspoon minced garlic

12 kari leaves or 2 bay leaves

2 tablespoons tomato paste

1 teaspoon tamarind paste (see page 216)
   or lemon juice

1/2 cup coconut milk, light cream,
   or low-fat milk

Coarse salt to taste

1. Place the fish on a plate. Combine the curry powder and red pepper and rub over the fish. Heat 2 tablespoons of the oil in a large heavy nonstick sauté pan until hot. Lightly dust the fish with flour and add to the oil. Cook until the fish is lightly browned, about 1 minute. Do not fully cook the fish. Return the fish to the plate and set aside.

2. Wipe the pan clean and add the remaining oil. When the oil is hot, add the mustard seeds and cover the pan with the lid because the seeds will pop and spatter. When the sputtering subsides, add the onion, garlic, and kari leaves. Cook until the onions are soft, about 3 minutes. Stir in 2 cups water, the tomato paste, and tamarind paste and boil the sauce until reduced and thick, about 5 minutes. Add the coconut milk, salt, and the fish. Cook until the sauce is piping hot and fish is heated through.

3. Serve warm, at room temperature, or cold, straight from the refrigerator.

GOAN WARM MUSSEL SALAD

Tisru

In this salad from Goa, once a Portuguese colony, coconut mellows the spices and har-monizes them with the mussels. Tisru is traditionally served with sweet buttery dinner rolls for mopping up the sauce. Plain rice or Indian bread would also pair well.

SERVES 4

2 tablespoons vegetable oil

1 cup finely chopped onion

1 tablespoon finely shredded fresh ginger

1 tablespoon ground coriander

1 teaspoon turmeric

$1/2$ to 1 teaspoon ground red pepper

$1/2$ cup coconut milk, fresh (see page 211)
    or canned

Coarse salt to taste

4 pounds mussels (about 4 dozen),
    scrubbed clean

Juice of 1 small lemon

2 tablespoons chopped fresh coriander
    (cilantro) leaves and tender stems

2 tablespoons grated unsweetened coconut
    (optional)

1. Place the oil and onions in a deep pot over high heat and cook, stirring, until they begin to brown, about 5 minutes. Lower the heat and stir in the ginger, coriander, turmeric, and red pepper. Cook for 1 minute. Stir in the coconut milk, salt, and mussels and bring to a boil.

2. Steam, covered, until the mussels open, about 7 minutes. Transfer the mussels and the sauce to a deep platter.

3. Sprinkle with lemon juice, fresh coriander and coconut. Serve immediately.

PAN-GRILLED SCALLOPS
with Ajowan

Bhoni Machi

This is one of the mildest, most delicate, and most elegant preparations from the coastal city of Bombay. Traditionally, pomfret, a white fish, is used, but scallops work beautifully. Serve the scallops with Green Pea Pilaf (page 80) and Curried Eggplant with Chutney (page 166).

SERVES 4

1 1/2 pounds scallops, preferably bay scallops

1/4 teaspoon ajowan seeds

1/4 teaspoon crushed red pepper

1 teaspoon minced garlic

1 tablespoon lemon juice

2 tablespoons minced fresh coriander (cilantro)
    leaves and tender stems

1 tablespoon minced basil

1 1/2 tablespoons vegetable oil

1. Put the scallops in a bowl. Combine the ajowan, red pepper, garlic, lemon juice, fresh coriander, basil, and oil and rub over the scallops.

2. Heat a large heavy nonstick sauté pan over high heat. When the pan is very hot, add the scallops and cook, shaking and tossing, until they turn ivory white and opaque, about 2 minutes, for bay scallops, 3 minutes for sea scallops

3. Serve immediately.

120

MOGHUL SHRIMP IN CREAM SAUCE

Malai Jheenga

Shrimp in cream sauce is a classic Moghul preparation. The unique flavor and creamy consistency of the dish comes from coconut milk. Scallops, lobster, crab, conch, and fish can be used in place of shrimp. Saffron Pilaf (page 84) or Flame-roasted Puffy Bread (page 46) would be good to serve with it.

SERVES 4

$1/4$ cup vegetable oil

1 cup finely chopped red onions

$1/2$ cup finely chopped shallots

2 bay leaves

$1/2$ teaspoon fennel seeds, crushed

4 whole cloves

2 teaspoons ground coriander

$1/4$ teaspoon turmeric

$1/4$ to $1/2$ teaspoon ground red pepper

1 pound medium shrimp, peeled and deveined

1 cup coconut milk, fresh (see page 211)
    or canned, or light cream

Coarse salt to taste

2 tablespoons heavy cream (optional)

1. Heat the oil in a medium saucepan over medium-high heat and add the onion, shallots, bay leaves, fennel, cloves, coriander, turmeric, and red pepper. Cook, stirring often, until the onion begins to brown, about 5 minutes. Add the shrimps and sauté until they begin to curl and turn pink, 2 to 3 minutes. Stir in the coconut milk and cook until the sauce is bubbling hot. Season with salt and add heavy cream, if desired.

2. Serve immediately.

MALABAR COCONUT SHRIMP

Konjupa

This dish is from Malabar, the sultry coastal region along the southwestern shores of India. Konjupa are tiny shrimps found in the local waters. They are cooked in coconut sauce with fresh ginger, green chiles, and cumin. The Malabar people like their konjupa very hot but you can tone down the heat by reducing the number of chiles. Serve them with Semolina Pilaf (page 86) and Curry-scented Mushrooms (page 168).

SERVES 4

3 tablespoons vegetable oil

1 teaspoon mustard seeds

1 teaspoon chopped garlic

1 cup finely chopped red onion

1 teaspoon cumin seeds, crushed

2 tablespoons shredded fresh ginger

2 to 8 green chiles, stemmed, seeded and shredded, to taste

2 kari leaves or 2 tablespoons chopped fresh coriander (cilantro) leaves and tender stems

2 cups coconut milk, fresh (see page 211) or canned

1¹/₂ pounds medium shrimp, peeled and deveined

Coarse salt to taste

1. Heat the oil in a large heavy nonstick sauté pan over medium-high heat. When the oil is hot, add the mustard seeds and cover the pan with the lid because the seeds will pop and spatter. When the sputtering subsides, add the garlic and onion. Cook stirring occasionally, until the onions begin to color, about 6 minutes. Stir in the cumin, ginger, chiles, kari leaves (if using), and coconut milk and bring to a boil. Cook, uncovered, until the sauce is thickened, about 8 minutes.

2. Add the shrimps and cook, stirring constantly, until they curl up and turn pink, about 3 minutes. Add salt. If you are using fresh coriander, add it now.

3. Serve immediately.

123

PARSI BREADED SHRIMP
in Green Paste

Jheenga Patia

Parsis like their food very hot. They would use chiles like habaneros, jalapeños, or Thai bird peppers. I personally cannot, and do not, consume such fiery concoctions. I like a moderate flavorful heat that dances on my palate. Accordingly, I would use a combination of chiles, mostly Anaheims with an arbol or two thrown in. Accompany the shrimp with a chutney such as Nectarine Chutney with Walnuts and Saffron (pages 194–195).

SERVES 4

1 1/2 pounds jumbo shrimp

GREEN PASTE

1 cup (lightly packed) fresh coriander (cilantro)
    leaves and tender stems

1/2 cup mint leaves

1/2 cup grated unsweetened coconut

1/4 cup lemon juice

5 cloves garlic, peeled

2 to 8 green chiles, stemmed, to taste

1 tablespoon sugar

Coarse salt to taste

Vegetable oil, for shallow frying

2 large eggs, lightly beaten

3 cups dried bread crumbs

1. Peel and devein the shrimp, leaving the tails on, and butterfly them. Rinse and pat dry on towels. To prevent the shrimp from curling during cooking, thread a toothpick along the length of each one. Set aside.

2. Combine all the ingredients for the green paste in a food processor or electric blender. Process into a paste and transfer to a bowl. Add shrimp to the green paste and toss to coat thoroughly.

3. Pour the oil to a depth of $1/2$ inch into a large skillet and heat to 375° over medium-high heat. Dip the shrimps first in the beaten eggs and then in bread crumbs. Slip them into the hot oil, in batches if necessary, and fry, turning, until the shrimps are cooked through and the coating is golden, about 3 minutes. Drain on paper towels.

4. Arrange the shrimp on a platter and serve with a chutney.

125

LOBSTER
with Spice Butter

Bagda Jingri

Cooking fish or shellfish with Panch Phoron *is a popular technique throughout eastern India. The spices are first fried in oil and then simmered in liquid to produce a highly fragrant spicy-floral broth for cooking the fish or shellfish. Although it is not traditional, I like to add a little tomato paste to the sauce. In addition to lending a piquant undertone, it helps round out the flavor. You can use crab, scallops, mussels, clams, shrimp, kingfish, sea bass, or haddock in place of the lobster.*

SERVES 4

3/4 pound cooked lobster meat

8 small red new potatoes

1 pound eggplant, preferably small Italian
　　or long Japanese eggplant

2 tablespoons mustard oil (see page 214)
　　or vegetable oil

1 1/2 teaspoons *Panch Phoron* (see page 8)

1 teaspoon turmeric

Coarse salt to taste

1 tablespoon tomato paste

1 to 4 green chiles, stemmed, seeded,
　　and shredded, to taste

2 tablespoons chopped fresh coriander
　　(cilantro) leaves and tender stems

1. Pick over the lobster meat and cut it into large pieces. Scrub the potatoes and peel partially. Prick all over with a fork. If using tiny Italian eggplants, leave them whole. Otherwise, cut the eggplant into $1^1/_2$-inch pieces.

2. Heat the oil in a large saucepan over medium-high heat. If you are using mustard oil, let it smoke for a moment to rid it of its pungency. When the oil is hot add the *Panch Phoron*. When the spices have turned several shades darker, add the turmeric, the potatoes and eggplant and mix well. Fry the vegetables, turning until they are well coated with oil, about 6 minutes.

3. Add 2 cups water and salt. Cover and cook over medium heat until the vegetables are tender, about 20 minutes. Stir in the tomato paste and chiles, and then fold in the lobster meat. Cook until heated through.

4. Sprinkle with fresh coriander and serve.

127

CHICKEN
AND POULTRY

Ask any Indian cook which meat is the most highly esteemed and he will tell you chicken because it is the most adaptable to Indian flavors. Among the best Indian chicken preparations are Tandoori Chicken and Chicken Biriyani. In the Indian way of cooking, the skin is always removed and discarded so that the spices can penetrate better into the meat. For best results, use small chickens or Cornish hens, preferably free range; they are more flavorful than big factory-farm birds.

In India, duck is treated as game, hence its use is restricted to only certain communities. The preparations have a festive tone and are reserved for special occasions. The recipe included in this book is just such a standout dish (see page 140).

CHICKEN CURRY

Murgh Masala

A Punjabi specialty from North India, this chicken curry is fragrant with cumin and fresh coriander. It is this distinctive aroma that is often associated with Indian food and that has captured the hearts and palates of people around the globe. This curry can also be made with other birds. Serve it with a rice dish or bread.

SERVES 4

1 chicken (3 pounds), cut into 8 to 10 pieces
and skinned

1 1/2 cups finely chopped onion

2 tablespoons grated or crushed fresh ginger

1 tablespoon minced garlic

1 tablespoon paprika

1/2 teaspoon ground red pepper

1 1/2 pounds ripe tomatoes, pureed with skin

Coarse salt to taste

2 teaspoons ground toasted cumin seeds
or Garam Masala (page 7)

1/2 cup finely chopped fresh coriander
(cilantro) leaves and tender stems

130

1. Heat a large heavy nonstick sauté pan over medium-high heat. Add the chicken pieces and sauté, turning until they lose their pink color and are seared, about 5 minutes. Add the onion, ginger, and garlic. Sauté, stirring, until the onion is lightly browned, about 8 minutes. It will brown unevenly, which is as it should be for the complex flavoring of the finished sauce. Add the paprika, red pepper, tomatoes, and salt.

2. Pour 1 cup water over the chicken and bring to a boil. Reduce the heat and simmer, covered, until the chicken is very tender, about 30 minutes. If the sauce is too thin, increase the heat and boil rapidly, uncovered, until it reduces to the desired consistency (like a pasta sauce). Stir in the cumin and half of the fresh coriander and transfer to a warm serving dish.

3. Sprinkle with the remaining coriander and serve.

131

CHICKEN IN CREAM SAUCE

Makhani Murgh

Also known as butter chicken, this dish is made by braising pieces of day-old grilled chicken, preferably tandoori style, in a creamy tomato sauce. Green Pea Pilaf (page 80) or the Baked Tandoori Bread (page 48) make an excellent accompaniment.

SERVES 4

1 recipe Tandoori Chicken (page 90),
    or 2 small roasted chickens, cut into
    serving pieces and skinned

4 tablespoons unsalted butter

2 teaspoons ground cumin

SAUCE

2 cups tomato puree

1 cup heavy cream

$^1/_4$ cup julienned fresh ginger

$^1/_2$ cup finely chopped fresh coriander (cilantro)
    leaves and tender stems

Coarse salt and black pepper to taste

132

1. Melt 2 tablespoons of the butter in a large heavy nonstick sauté pan over medium-high heat. Add the chicken pieces, sprinkle with the cumin, and sauté, turning, for 3 minutes. Add the ingredients for the sauce and simmer until the chicken absorbs some of the sauce and becomes meltingly tender, 15 minutes. Stir in the remaining butter. (*The dish may be made ahead and refrigerated for up to 2 days. Reheat it and check the seasonings, adding more pepper and chopped fresh coriander, if necessary.*)

2. Transfer to a warm dish and serve.

NOTE: For a hotter-tasting dish, fold in up to 4 green chiles, stemmed and minced with seeds, into the sauce.

133

CHICKEN BIRIYANI

Murgh Biriyani

A biriyani is a Moghul rice casserole similar to a pilaf, in which a korma, a rich and aromatic braised preparation, is layered with basmati rice and baked. An interesting touch I have added to this biriyani is mango chutney, which makes the casserole intriguingly spicy. Biriyani is a very satisfying one-dish meal. All you need to complete the meal is a green salad.

SERVES 4

1 recipe Moghul Chicken Korma (page 135).

1/4 cup Chicken Stock (page 36), milk,
 or water

2 tablespoons Mango Chutney, homemade
 (page 192) or storebought, finely chopped

1 recipe cooked rice

1/4 cup dark raisins

Coarse salt to taste

2 tablespoons toasted sliced almonds

1. Place the rack in the middle of the oven and preheat the oven to 350°.

2. Combine the chicken korma, stock, and mango chutney in an ovenproof dish. Carefully fold in the rice and raisins. Season with salt and cover the dish. Place in the oven for 30 minutes, or until the *biriyani* is piping hot and the flavors have blended through. Transfer to a warm platter, garnish with the almonds, and serve.

**Parsi Breaded Shrimp in
Green Paste** and **Nectarine Chutney
with Walnuts and Saffron**

Spring Smoked Salmon Kedgeree with Dill

Country Captain

Roast Duck with Cinnamon-Plum Glaze and
Pan-roasted Green Beans with Five Spices

Lamb Curry with Zucchini served
over **Green Chile Corn Bread**

Pork Vindaloo with **Basmati Rice** and **Indian Wilted Spinach**

Braised Chickpeas
with Spicy Sauce

Spiced Tea

MOGHUL CHICKEN KORMA

Murgh Korma

Korma is traditionally a mild creamy preparation but you can make it spicy by adding ground red pepper if you like. Serve it with Saffron Pilaf (page 84) or stuffed bread. A common use of korma is in biriyani, *the Moghul rice-and-meat casserole.*

SERVES 4

> 1 pound skinless and boneless chicken breast
>
> 1/4 cup vegetable oil
>
> 1 1/2 cups finely chopped onion
>
> 1 teaspoon ground cardamom
>
> 1 cup yogurt, lightly beaten
>
> Coarse salt to taste
>
> 2 teaspoons *Garam Masala* (page 7),
>   or 1 tablespoon ground coriander
>
> 1/4 cup heavy cream or milk
>
> 2 tablespoons toasted sliced almonds

1. Cut the chicken into 1-inch-wide strips. Cut each strip into 1/2-inch pieces. Set aside.

2. Heat the oil in a large heavy nonstick sauté pan over medium-high heat. Add the onions and cardamom. If you are using coriander, add it now. Cook until the onion begins to color, about 5 minutes. Add the chicken and continue to cook until it loses its pink color, about 4 minutes.

3. Stir in the yogurt and salt and bring the sauce to a boil. Reduce the heat and simmer, covered, until the chicken is tender and the sauce is reduced and thick, about 15 minutes. If the sauce is too thin, increase the heat and boil it, uncovered, until reduced to the desired consistency. Mix in the *Garam Masala* and cream and heat thoroughly. Transfer to a warm dish

4. Sprinkle with almonds and serve.

COUNTRY CAPTAIN

Kapitan

An Anglo-Indian specialty, Country Captain is essentially leftover meat warmed in a curry-and-vegetable sauce. It is an easy and quick technique that produces delicious results. You can also make this dish with leftover Roast Duck with Cinnamon-Plum Glaze (page 140), Tandoori Chicken (page 90), or any other roast poultry or meat.

SERVES 2

3/4 pound leftover cooked chicken meat

3 tablespoons unsalted butter

1 teaspoon finely chopped garlic

2 teaspoons Curry Powder (page 6)

1 1/2 cups chopped onion

2 teaspoons all-purpose flour

1 teaspoon Worcestershire sauce

1/3 cup heavy cream or Chicken Stock
    (page 36)

1 green bell pepper, cored and julienned

1 red bell pepper, cored and julienned

1/2 cup of 1-inch cubes pineapple

1/4 cup roasted cashews or slivered almonds
    (optional)

Freshly ground black pepper

1. Cut the chicken into 1 1/2-inch pieces.

2. Heat the butter in a large heavy nonstick sauté pan over medium-high heat. Add the garlic, Curry Powder, and onion, and cook, stirring occasionally, for 2 minutes or until the vegetables are barely soft. Add the flour and cook, stirring, for 1 minute. Stir in the Worcestershire sauce and cream and bring the sauce to a boil.

3. Add the green and red bell peppers. Reduce the heat to medium and cook, stirring and tossing, for 5 minutes or until the vegetables are barely soft. Fold in the chicken and cook until heated through. Fold in the pineapple. Transfer to a serving platter.

4. Sprinkle with pepper and scatter the cashews or almonds on top, if desired, and serve immediately.

137

CORNISH HEN VINDALOO

Vindaloo

Vindaloo is a hot and spicy dish generally associated with Goa, the former Portuguese colony on India's western coast. Vindaloos come in a range of spiciness, from moderate to blisteringly hot—the secret to their deliciousness in the spicing. Sweet cinnamon, cloves, anise, and shallots not only round out the flavors, but temper the heat to a very pleasant spark. Vindaloo is traditionally served with plain rice, although a mild pilaf is also a nice accompaniment, as is some bread and a fruity yogurt salad.

SERVES 4

2 Cornish hens (about 1 1/4 to 1 3/4 pound each)

3 tablespoons mustard oil (see page 214)
    or vegetable oil

3/4 cup finely chopped shallots

1 tablespoon minced garlic

2 teaspoons ground red pepper

3/4 teaspoon ground cinnamon

1/2 teaspoon ground cloves

1/4 teaspoon ground anise

1 tablespoon tomato paste

1 tablespoon prepared mustard

1 teaspoon maple syrup

Coarse salt to taste

138

1. Split the Cornish hens in half and remove the skin and all visible fat. Heat 1 tablespoon of the oil in a large heavy nonstick sauté pan over high heat. If you are using the mustard oil, let it smoke for a moment to rid it of its pungency. Reduce the heat, add the hens, and cook, turning, until they lose their pink color, about 5 minutes. Using a slotted spoon, remove them from the pan and transfer to a bowl.

2. Add the remaining oil to the pan. Add the shallots and garlic and cook, stirring occasionally, until the shallots are browned, about 10 minutes. Stir in the red pepper, cinnamon, cloves, and anise. Add the tomato paste, mustard, maple syrup, 1 1/2 cups water, the hens, and salt. Bring to a boil.

3. Lower the heat and cook, covered, for 35 minutes, or until the hens are very tender. (*The vindaloo may be prepared ahead and refrigerated for up to 4 days or frozen. In fact, the flavors improve with standing. It is also easier to remove the excess fat, which congeals at the top, when the dish is cold.*)

4. Transfer the vindaloo to a warm dish and serve.

Variations: ────────────────────────────

PORK VINDALOO:

Use 4 pork chops (about 2 pounds), trimmed of excess fat, in place of the Cornish hens. Increase the cooking time to 1 1/4 hours.

BEEF OR LAMB VINDALOO:

Use 1 1/2 pounds boneless lean beef or lamb, cut into 1 1/2-inch pieces, in place of the hens. Increase the cooking time to 1 3/4 hours.

VEGETABLE VINDALOO:

Replace the hens with 6 cups mixed vegetables, such as cauliflower, carrots, green beans, green peas, turnips, eggplant, and/or potatoes, cut into 2 × 1 × 1-inch pieces.

139

ROAST DUCK
with Cinnamon-Plum Glaze

Battak Roosht

Gloriously glazed to a rich mahogany, this cinnamon-laced roast duck can form the centerpiece of the most Western of dinners. Traditionally the roast does not have a watercress garnish, but I like to use it to contrast the sweet flavor and add more complexity. It goes very well with Green Pea Pilaf (page 80) or Saffron Pilaf (page 84).

SERVES 4

1 duck (4 to 5 pounds), excess fat removed

Coarse salt and black pepper

2 tablespoons unsalted butter

1 cup (about 15) shallots, peeled

2 sticks (3 inches) cinnamon

4 large purple plums, sliced

¹/₃ cup damson plum jam

¹/₄ teaspoon ground cinnamon

¹/₄ teaspoon ground ginger

1 bunch (6 to 7 ounces) watercress, for garnish
(optional)

1. Preheat the oven to 425°.

2. Rinse the duck and pat dry with paper towels. Rub salt and pepper all over the duck, inside and out.

3. Melt the butter in a large heavy nonstick sauté pan over medium-high heat. Add the shallots and the cinnamon sticks and fry, tossing frequently, until the shallots are lightly browned, about 10 minutes. Add the plums and cook, tossing, until coated with butter and heated through, about 1 minute. Spoon the cinnamon-plum-shallot mixture into the cavity of the duck. Sew or skewer closed.

4. Pour 1 cup water into a shallow roasting pan. Set the duck on its side on a rack in the pan. Roast for 45 minutes, turning every 15 minutes, first to the second side and then breast up.

5. Reduce the oven temperature to 350°. Combine the plum jam with the ground cinnamon and ginger. Brush the duck with some of the spiced jam. Continue to roast, turning occasionally and brushing with plum jam, until the duck is deep mahogany colored and tender, about 1 hour.

6. To serve, carve the duck into 4 portions and scoop out the stuffing. Spread the watercress on a serving platter, if you are using it. Arrange the duck in the center and surround with shallots and plum slices and cinnamon sticks. Serve immediately.

MEAT

THE Moghuls are credited with introducing some of the greatest meat dishes of Indian cooking. Lamb Curry with Apricots, Lamb with Spinach, and Kid Braised in a Fragrant Cream Sauce are just few examples. The meat most frequently used in Indian cooking is lamb or goat meat. This is because the religious taboos of the Hindus prevent them from eating beef, and those of the Muslims prevent them from eating pork.

Except for Beef Frazer, which is made with leftover roast beef, dishes in this chapter can be prepared ahead and refrigerated. In fact, the flavor improves with standing. They can also be frozen. Defrost slowly in the refrigerator before reheating.

You can use any cut of meat as long as the skin and fat is trimmed away so that flavorings can penetrate into the meat. Although not traditional, pork and veal can be substituted in recipes calling for lamb or beef.

Lamb Curry

Gosht Masala

The most popular of all curries, this one can be enjoyed with a simple bowl of rice or some bread. In place of lamb, you can substitute beef, veal, pork, or goat meat. Accompany Lamb Curry with Green Pea Pilaf (page 80) or Flaky Parsley Pinwheel Bread (page 58) and a yogurt salad such as Cool Cucumber and Yogurt Salad (page 184).

SERVES 4

1 1/2 pounds boneless lean leg of lamb, cut into
 1 1/2-inch pieces

3 tablespoons vegetable oil

2 cups finely chopped onion

1 tablespoon grated fresh ginger

2 teaspoons minced garlic

2 teaspoons ground cumin

1 tablespoon ground coriander

1/2 teaspoon ground red pepper

1 tablespoon paprika

1 teaspoon turmeric

1 cup pureed tomato

Coarse salt to taste

1/3 cup chopped fresh coriander (cilantro)
 leaves and tender stems

1. Heat a heavy nonstick saucepan over high heat. Add the lamb and 1 tablespoon of the oil. Sear the meat, turning and tossing, until nicely browned all over. Transfer the meat to a plate.

2. Add the remaining oil and the onion to the pan and cook, stirring often, until the onion is browned, about 15 minutes. Stir in the ginger, garlic, cumin, coriander, red pepper, paprika, and turmeric and cook for 3 minutes more. Add the tomato purée, meat, salt, and enough water to fully cover the meat, about

1 1/2 cups. Bring to a boil. Reduce the heat and simmer, covered, for 1 1/2 hours, or until the meat is cooked and very tender. Let the curry rest for at least 30 minutes and reheat it before serving. *(This dish may be made ahead and refrigerated for up to 3 days or frozen. In fact, the flavors improve with standing. If frozen defrost and reheat slowly until piping hot.)*

3. Sprinkle with fresh coriander and serve.

Variation:

LAMB CURRY WITH APRICOTS:

Sauté 1 pound ripe apricots, peeled, pitted, and cut into thick wedges, in 1 tablespoon vegetable oil in a large sauté pan until streaked with brown and glazed, about 6 minutes. Arrange the apricots on top of the curry before serving.

LAMB CURRY WITH OKRA:

Fry 4 ounces okra, stemmed and left whole, in 2 tablespoons oil in a large sauté pan until lightly browned and partially cooked, about 10 minutes. Add to the curry during the last 10 minutes of cooking.

LAMB CURRY WITH POTATOES:

Add 4 to 6 scrubbed small waxy or new potatoes during the last 30 minutes of cooking.

LAMB CURRY WITH ZUCCHINI:

Add 2 medium zucchini, diced into 1 × 1 × 1/2-inch pieces, during the last 15 minutes of cooking.

Lamb
with Spinach

Saag Gosht

Spinach is eaten extensively in India; it is inexpensive and available year round. It is used to flavor breads or yogurt salads or to make dumplings or soup, or is stir-fried in a fragrant oil. In this dish it is used to enhance the sauce. In place of spinach, you can substitute an equal quantity of another green, or a combination of other greens, such as mustard greens, Swiss chard, or beet tops. Accompany the curry with bread or rice.

SERVES 4

1 cup (packed) chopped cooked spinach,
    fresh or frozen, thawed

3 tablespoons vegetable oil

¹/₂ cup finely chopped onions

2 teaspoons *Garam Masala* (page 7)
    or ground cumin

1 to 2 teaspoons minced green chiles (optional)

1 recipe Lamb Curry (page 144)

1. Squeeze the spinach to remove excess moisture. Set aside.

2. Heat the oil in a large sauté pan. When the oil is hot, add the onion and cook until brown, about 8 minutes. Stir in the *Garam Masala* and chiles, if using. Add the spinach and sauté for 3 minutes. (*The spinach mixture may be made ahead and refrigerated up to 2 days. Stir the spinach into the curry just before serving.*)

3. Add the seasoned spinach to the curry, stir well to mix and serve.

CURRY
with Brussels Sprouts

Mutton Curry

This curry is an Anglo-Indian classic from the town of Ootacamund (affectionately known as Ooty) in the Blue Mountain range of southern India. Brussels sprouts, introduced by the British in the nineteenth century, grow abundantly there. They are a pleasant addition to curry, giving it a very earthy wholesome taste. Mixed green salad and bread will complete the meal. For hot curry, add minced green chiles to taste with the cream.

SERVES 4

1 pound boneless lean lamb, cut into
    1 1/2-inch pieces

3 tablespoons all-purpose flour

1/4 cup vegetable oil

1 cup finely chopped shallots

2 tablespoons Curry Powder (page 6)

1 tablespoon prepared mustard

1 cup Chicken Stock (page 36)

Coarse salt to taste

1 pound Brussels sprouts, trimmed

1/4 cup heavy cream

Black pepper

1. Dust the meat with flour. Heat 2 tablespoons of the oil in a large heavy non-stick sauté pan over high heat. Add the meat and sauté, turning, until browned on all sides, about 3 minutes. Transfer the meat to a plate.

2. Add the remaining oil to the pan along with the shallots and Curry Powder. Cook, stirring, until the spices give off an aroma. Return the meat to the pan. Add the mustard, stock, and salt and bring to a boil. Reduce the heat and simmer, covered, stirring occasionally, for 1 hour. Fold in the brussels sprouts and continue to cook for 25 minutes more, or until they are tender but still firm. Stir in the cream.

3. Sprinkle with black pepper and serve.

KID BRAISED IN
a Fragrant Cream Sauce

Aab Gosht

This Moghul specialty from Pakistan is an elegant, rich dish generally reserved for company. Goat meat is first braised in an aromatic cream sauce, then dressed with garlic-herb butter. Veal or lamb may be substituted for the goat meat. This dish is best served with a fragrant pilaf such as Peach and Walnut Basmati Pilaf (page 76) or Saffron Pilaf (page 84).

SERVES 4 TO 6

1 cup light cream

1 cup chopped onion

3 tablespoons blanched almonds

1 teaspoon ground cardamom

$1/4$ teaspoon grated nutmeg

$1/4$ teaspoon ground cloves

$1/4$ teaspoon ground anise

$1^1/2$ pounds boneless goat meat or veal,
    cut into 1-inch pieces

Coarse salt to taste

2 tablespoons *usli ghee* (see page 216)
    or clarified butter

1 teaspoon minced garlic

$1/2$ teaspoon black pepper

2 tablespoons minced mint

2 tablespoons minced frest coriander (cilantro)
    leaves and tender stems

$1/2$ cup heavy cream (optional)

1. Put the light cream, onion, and almonds in the workbowl of an electric blender or food processor. Process until liquefied. Mix in the cardamom, nutmeg, cloves, and anise.

2. Combine the pureed mixture with the meat and salt in a large, heavy nonstick saucepan and bring to a boil. Lower the heat and simmer, partially covered, for 1 hour, or until the meat is tender and the sauce is thick enough to coat the meat. Check often and stir to prevent sticking and burning.

3. Heat the *usli ghee* in a small frying pan over medium-high heat until hot. Add the garlic, black pepper, mint, and fresh coriander. As soon as the garlic releases aroma, remove the pan from heat. Immediately pour the herb mixture over the meat. Add heavy cream, if desired. Mix well and serve.

DRY-COOKED SPICY GROUND BEEF

Sookha Keema

Dry-cooked ground meat is one of the most basic Moghul preparations. It may be served as a main dish in its own right or be made more substantial by combining it with cooked vegetables such as potatoes, sweet potatoes, turnips, or plantain. It is the basis for the classic filling for the Moghul stuffed bread (see page 60). For a quick sandwich, stuff pita pockets or taco shells with the beef, topping it with sliced tomatoes and lettuce. The following recipe, developed in my cooking school, is quick, easy and light. It produces just as good results as one using the conventional method.

SERVES 4

1½ pounds lean ground sirloin or round

3 tablespoons vegetable oil

4 teaspoons ground coriander

2 teaspoons ground cumin

1 teaspoon turmeric

½ teaspoon ground red pepper

1½ cups finely chopped onion

2 tablespoons minced garlic

2 tablespoons grated or crushed fresh ginger

2 cups chopped tomatoes, fresh or canned

Coarse salt to taste

1. Heat a heavy saucepan over medium-high heat. Add the beef and cook, stirring, until it is no longer pink and begins to brown. Transfer to a colander, drain, and return to the pan.

2. Add the oil, coriander, cumin, turmeric, red pepper, onion, garlic, and ginger. Cook, stirring, until the onion looks soft and glazed, about 10 minutes. Add the tomatoes, 2 cups water, and salt and bring to a boil. Reduce the heat and sim-

mer, uncovered, until all the moisture evaporates, about 30 minutes. Check periodically and stir to prevent sticking and burning.

3. Serve immediately or set aside for other uses.

NOTE: For a smoother texture, transfer the cooked beef to a food processor and process briefly. Do not overprocess as it will turn into an unpleasant paste.

MOGHUL GROUND MEAT STEW

Keema

This spicy Indian stew is similar in appearance to the Mexican chili. It is a great party dish since it is easy to make in quantity and it keeps well at room temperature. The stew is generally accompanied with Indian Salsa (page 196) and Deep-fried Puffy Bread (page 52) or Mint Rice (page 83).

SERVES 4

> 1 recipe Dry-cooked Spicy Ground Beef
> (page 152).
> 1 cup tomato puree

1. Prepare the beef through Step 2 of the recipe. Stir in the tomato puree and as much water as needed to make a thick chili-like mixture.

2. Reheat and serve hot.

153

GROUND MEAT
with Smoked Eggplant

Keema Baigan

For the purist, here is Keema made the traditional way, in which the onions are browned before the meat and spices are added. For a special twist, I have added smoky roasted eggplant to the finished Keema; it lends flavor and body to the sauce. You can substitute lamb, goat meat, pork, or chicken for the beef. This Keema is also delicious made with venison, buffalo, or moose meat. Serve it with a simple bread like chapati *(see page 44) or with Mint Rice (page 83).*

SERVES 4

2 medium eggplants (about 1 1/2 pounds)

1 tablespoon lemon juice

2 cups chopped onion

1 tablespoon chopped garlic

1/4 cup vegetable oil

1 pound lean ground sirloin or round

1 tablespoon *Garam Masala* (page 7)

Coarse salt to taste

2 cups peeled and chopped tomatoes

2 teaspoons grated fresh ginger

1/4 cup chopped fresh coriander (cilantro)
leaves and tender stems

1. Place the eggplant on a gas burner, at first stem side up then laying them on their sides, turning them every minute until they are fully charred and very soft, about 20 minutes. When cool enough to handle, carefully scrape the charred skin off. Rinse quickly under running cold water to wash away any clinging charred pieces and drain. Coarsely chop the pulp and put in a bowl. Stir in the lemon juice and set aside. (*The eggplant may be made ahead and refrigerated for up to 2 days or frozen. Defrost before proceeding with Step 3.*)

2. Put the onion, garlic, and oil in a large heavy saucepan. Cook over medium-high heat, stirring occasionally, until the onion is browned, about 15 minutes. Add the ground beef and continue to cook until it loses its pink color. Add 2 cups water and bring to a boil. Lower the heat and cook, covered, until the meat is tender and the sauce thickened, about 25 minutes. (*The meat may be refrigerated for up to 2 days or frozen. Defrost before proceeding with Step 3.*)

3. Stir in the *Garam Masala*, salt, tomatoes, ginger, fresh coriander, and eggplant. Heat thoroughly and serve.

NOTE: To roast eggplants in the oven, place them in a shallow baking dish and bake in a preheated 425° oven for 45 minutes, or until the eggplants are soft and limp and their skin entirely wrinkled.

BEEF FRAZER

Jhal Frazi

Named after Colonel Frazer, an important figure of the British Raj, this dish is a sauté of leftover roast beef with vegetables. It makes a great buffet dish and is also good for lunch, accompanied by plain rice and a vegetable like Curried Eggplant with Chutney (page 166).

SERVES 2

3/4 pound leftover roast beef

1 teaspoon ground cumin

2 teaspoons Curry Powder (page 6)

4 tablespoons unsalted butter

4 scallions, trimmed and shredded, both the
    green and white part

1 cup thin tomato wedges with skin

2 teaspoons prepared mustard

1/4 cup Chicken Stock (page 36)
    or water

Black pepper

2 tablespoons chopped fresh coriander
    (cilantro) leaves and tender stems

1. Cut the beef into 1-inch cubes. Sprinkle with the cumin and Curry Powder and rub in. Heat the butter in a large sauté pan over medium-high heat. When the butter melts, add the beef and scallions and sauté, turning, for 4 minutes, or until the beef is warmed through and begins to brown.

2. Increase the heat to high and add the tomatoes. Stir the mustard into the stock and pour over the beef. Cook until the tomatoes begin to soften, about 4 minutes.

3. Transfer to a platter, sprinkle with black pepper and coriander, and serve.

VEGETABLES, LEGUMES, EGGS, AND CHEESE

WITH over 700 million practicing vegetarians in India, it should come as no surprise that India is the ruling champion when it comes to vegetable cooking. Fresh, seasonal vegetables are prepared in myriad ways with intricate spicing and seasonings. Often the vegetables are flavored with only one or two spices to lend just a teasing fragrance. The spices are cooked in hot oil to make a spice-infused oil in which the vegetables are then cooked. Each Indian kitchen has its own preferred flavors and techniques, but generally speaking, those in the north commonly use cumin; those in the east, mustard; those in the south, kari; and those in the west, ajowan. Just about any vegetable can be prepared the Indian way, the popular ones are cauliflower, eggplant, potato, squash, green beans, and greens. Legumes, eggs, and homemade cheese, popular ingredients of the Indian vegetarian diets, are enjoyed by all.

GREEN BEENS
in Fenugreek Oil

Sem Bhaji

These green beans are flavored in style of Assam, where vegetables are often cooked in oil flavored with fenugreek, garlic shoots, and chiles. My maternal grandparents, who settled in Burma near the Assam border, particularly liked this dish made with green beans or with spinach, the traditional choices. Wonderful with tandoori meats, the beans are also good served cold with drinks.

SERVES 4

> 1 pound green beans
>
> 1 small bunch garlic shoots, or 6 scallions
>
> 1 tablespoon vegetable oil
>
> $1/4$ teaspoon fenugreek seeds
>
> $1/2$ teaspoon turmeric
>
> $1/2$ teaspoon finely chopped green chiles
>
> Coarse salt to taste

1. Trim the green beans and rinse in cold water. Trim the garlic shoots and cut into 4-inch-long pieces then quarter each lengthwise.

2. Heat the oil in a large heavy sauté pan over high heat. Add the fenugreek seeds and cook until they turn very dark brown, about 1 minute. Add the turmeric, green beans, and chiles. Fry the vegetables, turning and tossing, until lightly browned, about 5 minutes. Sprinkle with salt and $1/3$ cup water.

3. Reduce the heat and cook, covered, until soft, about 10 minutes. If the vegetables look a little moist, uncover and boil rapidly until dried and glazed.

4. Serve hot, at room temperature, or chilled.

161

BROCCOLI AND CARROTS
in Garlic-Turmeric Oil

Sabzi

This crisp sauté is great with fish, such as Steamed Fish in Herb Sauce (page 112). Since the dish may be served hot, cold, or at room temperature, it is perfect for a buffet or picnic. In India, vegetables cooked this way are usually served with flatbread to wrap around them.

SERVES 4

1 medium bunch broccoli (about 1 3/4 pounds)

2 medium carrots

3 tablespoons vegetable oil

10 large cloves garlic, peeled

1/2 teaspoon turmeric

1/2 teaspoon sugar

1/2 lime

162

1. Cut the broccoli into spears, leaving long stems attached to the florets and peel the stems. Peel and slice the carrots lengthwise into $1/4$-inch-wide strips.

2. Bring a large pot of water to a boil and add the broccoli and carrots. Blanch for about 2 minutes, drain, rinse under cold running water, and drain again.

3. Heat the oil in a large sauté pan over medium-high heat. Add the garlic cloves and sauté over medium heat until golden, about 6 minutes. Add the broccoli, carrots, and turmeric and sauté, stirring frequently, until the vegetables soften, about 6 minutes. Sprinkle with sugar and continue to sauté until the vegetables are lightly browned, about 2 minutes more.

4. To serve, pick the broccoli and carrots up with tongs and arrange them in a bouquet on a serving platter. Scatter the leftover garlic from the pan on top and sprinkle with lime juice. Serve hot, at room temperature, or chilled.

163

CAULIFLOWER
with Nigella in Ginger Oil

Adrak Gobhi

Of all the vegetables, it seems Indians like cauliflower the most. In this preparation, it is lightly spiced, then sautéed in a ginger-infused oil. This gives the dish a herbal fragrance without overpowering the delicate flavor of the cauliflower. It can be served with any spicy dish.

SERVES 4

1 medium head cauliflower (about 1 1/2 pounds)

2 tablespoons vegetable oil

2 tablespoons julienned fresh ginger

3/4 teaspoon nigella seeds or cumin seeds

1/2 teaspoon turmeric

Coarse salt to taste

1. Separate the cauliflower into small florets, cutting them with a knife if necessary. Peel the cauliflower stem and slice it into $1/4$-inch-thick rounds. Wash the cauliflower pieces in running cold water and drain.

2. Heat the oil in a large sauté pan over medium heat. When the oil is hot, add the ginger and let it sizzle in the oil for 1 minute. Add the nigella seeds, turmeric, and cauliflower. Sauté, turning and tossing, until evenly coated with the spices, about 3 minutes.

3. Stir in $1/2$ cup water and salt. Reduce the heat and cook, covered, until the cauliflower is fully cooked but still firm, about 10 minutes. Uncover, increase the heat and stir-fry until any excess moisture has evaporated and the cauliflower looks glazed.

Variation: ———————————————————————

For a hotter dish, stir in 2 chopped green chiles and/or $1/4$ teaspoon ground red pepper along with the nigella and turmeric.

165

CURRIED EGGPLANT
with Chutney

Bhuna Baigan

An old Anglo-Indian favorite, this curry-flavored eggplant is sweet and savory at the same time, perfect with tandoori meats or simple grilled chicken or sautéed fish. I also like to make a sandwich of it with lettuce and tomato for a satisfying vegetarian snack. The dish is good both hot and at room temperature.

SERVES 4

> 2 large (about 2 pounds) eggplants
>
> 1 medium onion, peeled and cut into
> ¼-inch slices
>
> 2 teaspoons Curry Powder (page 6)
>
> ¼ teaspoon ground ginger
>
> 3 tablespoons vegetable oil
>
> Coarse salt to taste
>
> 2 teaspoons lemon juice
>
> 2 tablespoons chutney, homemade
> or storebought

1. Bring a large pot of water to a boil. Cut the eggplant into 1-inch cubes Add the eggplant cubes to the boiling water and blanch for 1 minute. Drain and put in a bowl. Add the onion, Curry Powder, and ginger. Toss to mix.

2. Heat the oil in a large sauté pan over high heat. Add the eggplant and sauté, tossing frequently, for about 3 minutes. Reduce the heat and cook, uncovered, tossing, until the eggplant is tender, about 25 minutes. Turn off heat and stir in the salt, lemon juice and chutney.

CURRY-SCENTED MUSHROOMS

Khombi Bhaji

These garlicky, slightly spicy mushrooms are good as a nibble with drinks, as a sit-down first course, or even at breakfast with sausage and eggs. I particularly like them with a sautéed or fried dish like Parsi Breaded Shrimp in Green Paste (page 124) or Chicken Ginger Kebabs (page 92) and rice.

SERVES 4

2 tablespoons vegetable oil

1¹/₂ pounds white button mushrooms, halved
   or quartered if large

1 tablespoon Curry Powder (page 6)

1 tablespoon chopped garlic

¹/₄ teaspoon crushed red pepper flakes

¹/₄ teaspoon sugar

2 teaspoons lemon juice

2 tablespoons chopped fresh coriander
   (cilantro) leaves and tender stems

1. Heat the oil in a large heavy sauté pan over high heat. When the oil is hot, add the mushrooms and cook, turning and tossing, until lightly browned. Add the Curry Powder, garlic, red pepper, and sugar. Lower the heat and sauté, stirring, until the mushrooms are soft and glazed.

2. Sprinkle with lemon juice and fresh coriander and serve.

CUMIN POTATOES

Jeera Aloo

This is one the most popular everyday techniques for cooking vegetables in North India. It's so simple: cooked vegetables are pan-seared in a spice-infused oil. Any seasonal vegetable will work although starchy vegetables like potatoes, sweet potatoes, taro root, and plantains are preferred. The potatoes are great at breakfast or with grilled meats. For a vegetarian meal, roll them in a flatbread or stuff them in pita pockets with lettuce and tomato slices.

SERVES 4

> 1 1/2 pounds small waxy or new potatoes
>
> 1 tablespoon vegetable oil
>
> 1 teaspoon cumin seeds
>
> 1/2 teaspoon turmeric
>
> Coarse salt to taste
>
> 2 tablespoons minced fresh coriander (cilantro) leaves and tender stems

1. Boil the potatoes in their jackets until tender but not cracked open. Drain. When cool enough to handle, quarter the potatoes. Leave the skin on.

2. Heat the oil in a large heavy nonstick sauté pan over medium-high heat. Add the cumin seeds and sauté until they turn several shades darker, about 1 minute. Add the turmeric and potatoes and sauté, tossing frequently, until the potatoes are nicely browned, about 10 minutes.

3. Sprinkle with fresh coriander and serve hot, at room temperature, or cold.

Pan-roasted Potatoes
with Five Spices

Aloo Bhona

This is one of the basic ways of cooking vegetables in eastern India. The vegetables are first cooked in a broth scented with Panch Phoron, a blend of five spices, and then pan-roasted. Starchy vegetables, such as potatoes, are particularly well suited to this technique but you can use any seasonal vegetable, remembering to adjust the cooking time. For great flavor and color use purple or Yukon Gold potatoes. For a hotter dish, stir in 1 teaspoon chopped chiles or ¹/₂ teaspoon ground red pepper with the Panch Phoron.

Serves 4

2 tablespoons vegetable oil

1¹/₂ teaspoons *Panch Phoron* (page 8)

1¹/₂ pounds small waxy or new potatoes,
    left whole or halved

¹/₄ teaspoon powdered asafetida
    or minced garlic

Coarse salt and black pepper

Juice of ¹/₂ lemon

1. Heat the oil in a large heavy nonstick pan over medium-high heat. Add the *Panch Phoron* and sauté until the spices turn several shades darker. Add the potatoes and sprinkle with asafetida.

2. Fry the potatoes, turning and tossing, until evenly coated with spices and lightly browned, about 5 minutes. Stir in 1 cup water and bring to a boil. Reduce the heat and cook, covered, until the potatoes are tender, about 20 minutes. Uncover and pan-roast until the excess moisture has evaporated and the potatoes look browned.

3. Season with salt and pepper, sprinkle with lemon juice, and serve warm, at room temperature, or cold.

Variations:

PAN-ROASTED BABY EGGPLANT WITH FIVE SPICES:

Use 1 1/2 pounds small Italian eggplant, halved or quartered with the stem, in place of the potatoes. Reduce the cooking time to 15 minutes.

PAN-ROASTED GREEN BEANS WITH FIVE SPICES:

Use 1 pound fresh green butter beans, or asparagus, trimmed, in place of the potatoes. Reduce the cooking time to 15 minutes.

INDIAN WILTED SPINACH

Masial

A specialty of the central province of Bhopal, this wilted greens preparation is truly poor man's food. Freshly picked greens from the backyard are sautéed with chile and garlic. What gives the dish an added dimension of flavor is the mustard oil, a common cooking medium in the region. The dish, however, is delicious even without it. You can make this dish with other greens, such as chard, escarole, kale, and so forth. With these greens, you should blanch them before adding them to the hot oil and increase the cooking time to 6 minutes.

SERVES 4

3 tablespoons mustard oil (see page 214)
   or vegetable oil or a combination

2 teaspoons finely chopped garlic

$^1/_2$ teaspoon crushed red pepper flakes

2 pounds fresh spinach, stemmed and carefully
   washed

Coarse salt and black pepper

172

1. If using mustard oil, heat it in a skillet over high heat. Let the oil smoke for a moment to rid it of its pungency. Add the garlic and red pepper and immediately top them with the spinach. Stir quickly and constantly until the spinach is wilted, about 3 minutes. Season with salt and pepper just as the spinach begins to wilt. Cook, stirring, until the spinach is tender, about 2 minutes more.

2. Transfer to a small dish and serve immediately.

BRAISED CHICK PEAS
with Spicy Sauce

Chana Masala

Chick peas in a spicy ginger-tomato sauce can be served at brunch or lunch accompanied by Deep-fried Puffy Bread (page 52) and a sweet fruity chutney like the Peach Chutney with Walnuts and Saffron (page 194). Ajowan, a thyme-flavored spice, is usually added to chick pea preparations to help make them more digestible.

SERVES 4

3 tablespoons vegetable oil

2 teaspoons cumin seeds

$1/4$ teaspoon ajowan seeds or dried thyme

1 cup finely chopped onion

2 tablespoons grated fresh ginger

1 cup chopped tomato

2 tablespoons tomato paste

2 cups cooked or canned chick peas, drained

Black pepper and coarse salt

GARNISH

$1/4$ cup finely chopped fresh coriander (cilantro)
   leaves and tender stems

$1/4$ cup finely chopped onion

1 tablespoon chopped green chiles

1. Heat the oil in a large pan over medium-high heat. Add the cumin, ajowan, onion, and ginger. Cook, stirring often, until the onion turns light brown, about 8 minutes. Add the tomato, tomato paste, and chick peas.

2. Lower the heat and simmer, covered, for 15 minutes, or until the flavors have blended and the sauce is very thick. Sprinkle generously with black pepper and season with salt. (*This dish may be made ahead and refrigerated for up to 4 days or frozen. Defrost thoroughly before reheating. Check the seasonings, and if necessary, add up two teaspoons* Garam Masala *[page 7] to perk up the flavors.*)

3. Transfer to a warm dish and top with chopped fresh coriander and onions. Pass the chiles on the side.

Variation:

RED KIDNEY BEANS WITH SPICY SAUCE:

Substitute 2 cups cooked red kidney beans for the chick peas

New Delhi Spiced Lentils

Dal

Dal, *a puree of lentils flavored with spices and herbs, is served with all traditional Indian meals. Typically used as a sauce, dal is spooned over rice or grilled meat to add moisture to the meal. Thinned with low-fat milk, buttermilk or tomato juice, dal makes a refreshing soup. You can use yellow lentils, yellow split peas or yellow mung beans in place of red lentils. Yellow mung beans will take about the same time to cook, yellow lentils and split peas twice as long.*

SERVES 4

1 1/4 cups red lentils

1/2 teaspoon turmeric

Coarse salt to taste

SPICE BUTTER

3 tablespoons *usli ghee* (see page 216)
  or vegetable oil

1 teaspoon cumin seeds

4 large cloves garlic, peeled and thickly sliced

1/4 teaspoon ground red pepper

1/4 cup finely chopped fresh coriander (cilantro)
  leaves and tender stems

176

1. Put the lentils and turmeric in a saucepan. Add 3 cups water and bring to a boil. Reduce the heat and simmer, partially covered, until tender, about 20 minutes. Stir a few times during cooking to keep the lentils from sticking to the pan and burning. Add more water if necessary. Turn off the heat. The consistency should be like pea soup; if not, add more water. Add salt, cover, and set aside.

2. Heat the *usli ghee* in a small frying pan over medium-high heat. Add the cumin seeds and sauté until they turn several shades darker. Add the garlic and red pepper. Sauté until the garlic turn golden, about 1 minute.

3. Transfer the lentils to a warm dish. Pour the spice-infused butter over the lentils. Sprinkle with fresh coriander and serve.

CURRIED LENTILS
with Tomatoes and Zucchini

Sambaar Dal

Packed with vegetables, this dal *is like a hearty stew or ragout, a one-dish meal. Flavorings in this* dal *are kept to a minimum so that the natural flavors of the lentils and basmati rice with which it is generally served are not masked. You could also serve it with Semolina Pilaf (page 86).*

SERVES 4

> 1 cup yellow lentils or yellow split peas
>
> ¹/₂ teaspoon turmeric
>
> Coarse salt
>
> 1 cup chopped tomatoes

SPICED VEGETABLES

> 2 tablespoons vegetable oil
>
> 2 teaspoons Curry Powder (page 6)
>
> 2 teaspoons ground coriander
>
> 1 cup chopped shallots
>
> 1 cup chopped zucchini
>
> ¹/₄ cup chopped fresh coriander (cilantro) leaves and tender stems

1. Put the lentils and turmeric in a large saucepan. Add 3 cups water and bring to a boil. Reduce the heat and simmer, partially covered, until tender, about 35 minutes. Stir a few times during cooking to keep the lentils from sticking to the pan and burning. Add more water if necessary. Turn off the heat. Stir in the salt and tomatoes, cover and set aside.

2. Heat the oil in a large skillet over medium heat. Add the Curry Powder, coriander, shallots, and zucchini. Sauté until the vegetables begin to brown, about, 6 minutes. Reduce the heat and cook, covered, until the vegetables are tender, about 6 minutes. Add the vegetable mixture to the lentils and mix lightly. Check the seasonings and add salt if necessary. Heat through.

3. Sprinkle with fresh coriander and serve.

179

INDIAN-STYLE OMELET

Aamlait

Indians like everything spiced up. Not necessarily heavily, but a spice or two must be added to a dish for it be considered properly prepared. An omelet is no exception. Enriched with onions, tomatoes, chiles, and coriander, this omelet is spicy and delicious. Choose the chiles, mild to hot, according to your taste.

SERVES 1

> 2 large eggs
>
> 2 tablespoons finely chopped red onion
>
> 2 tablespoons finely chopped tomato
>
> 1 to 2 teaspoons chopped green chiles
>
> 2 tablespoons chopped fresh coriander
>   (cilantro) leaves and tender stems
>
> Coarse salt to taste
>
> 1 tablespoon *usli ghee* (see page 216)
>   or unsalted butter

1. Combine the eggs, red onion, tomato, chiles, fresh coriander, and salt in a bowl and beat until lightly frothy.

2. Heat the *usli ghee* in a large nonstick frying pan over medium-high heat. Add the egg mixture and spread, tilting and swirling, until it covers the entire bottom of the pan. Cook until the egg is set and the underside is lightly browned, about 1 1/2 minutes. Turn the omelet with a wide spatula and cook for 30 seconds, or until the second side is browned.

3. Transfer to a dinner plate and serve.

MASALA CHEESE SCRAMBLE

Paneer Bhorji

This is an Indian alternative to scrambled eggs made using the Indian cheese paneer. *Filled with fresh coriander, chiles, and tomatoes,* bhorji *is light and refreshing. Accompany it with any Indian bread.*

SERVES 2

> 1 cup *paneer* (see page 215), or 8 ounces
>   farmer cheese or tofu
>
> 1/8 teaspoon turmeric mixed with 2 teaspoons
>   water
>
> Coarse salt to taste
>
> 2 tablespoons *usli ghee* (page 216) or unsalted
>   butter
>
> 1/2 teaspoon cumin seeds
>
> 1/4 cup finely chopped red onion
>
> 1 teaspoon grated or crushed ginger
>
> 1 to 2 teaspoons chopped green chiles
>
> 1/2 cup finely chopped tomatoes, drained
>
> 1/4 cup chopped fresh coriander (cilantro)
>   leaves and tender stems

1. Place the *paneer* in a bowl. Sprinkle with turmeric and salt and set aside.

2. Heat the *usli ghee* in a large nonstick frying pan over medium-high heat. Add the cumin seeds and cook until the spice turns several shades darker. Add the onion, ginger, and chiles and cook until the onions are soft, about 3 minutes. Add the tomato and cheese and cook, stirring until the seasonings are evenly distributed in the cheese, about 5 minutes.

3. Fold in the fresh coriander and serve.

YOGURT SALADS, CHUTNEYS, AND CONDIMENTS

Yogurt salads, a combination of yogurt and vegetables, fruits, and nuts, provide the moisture that may be lacking in such foods as grilled kebabs, roasts, and tandoori chicken. Raitas, as these yogurt salads are called, are mellow and cooling, hence an important adjunct to spicy Indian food. Raitas can also be pureed and served as a dip, such as Roasted Pepper Dip or combined with cooked seafood or chicken in a salad like the Chicken and Roasted Pepper Chat.

Chutney, from the word *chatni*, which means licking good in Sanskrit is a spicy condiment that appears at most India meals. It is a unique Indian combination of fruits, seasonings, vinegar, and sugar with nearly unlimited variations of ingredients and texture.

Cool Cucumber and Yogurt Salad

Kheera Raita

Flavored in the classic New Delhi style with roasted cumin and mint leaves, this subtle raita is an ideal accompaniment to all Moghul dishes, northern curries and tandoori dishes.

Serves 4

> 1 cup yogurt
>
> 1 teaspoon minced mint
>
> Freshly ground black pepper and coarse salt
>   to taste
>
> 1 teaspoon sugar (optional)
>
> 2 medium-sized cucumbers, peeled, seeded
>   and grated
>
> 1/4 teaspoon toasted cumin seeds

184

Whip the yogurt, mint, pepper, salt, and sugar, if using, in a bowl until thoroughly blended. Stir in the cucumber and cumin seeds. Serve immediately or refrigerate.

Banana-Coconut Yogurt Salad

Kela Raita

This cool banana raita is an all-time favorite at wedding receptions and banquets. Indian cooks would use the small finger bananas or red bananas. They are sweeter and firmer than regular bananas and hold their shape better in a sauce. For best result, use firm, just ripe bananas with no spots.

Serves 4

2 cups yogurt

2 tablespoons sweetened grated coconut

$1/2$ teaspoon grated fresh ginger

$1/4$ teaspoon ground cardamom

1 teaspoon dried green peppercorns,
    or $1/4$ teaspoon ground white pepper

Coarse salt to taste

2 bananas, thinly sliced

Whip the yogurt, coconut, ginger, cardamom, green peppercorns, and salt in a bowl until thoroughly blended. Fold in the bananas. Refrigerate for at least 2 hours. Serve chilled.

185

Roasted Pepper
and Mint Yogurt Salad

Mirch Raita

This smoky raita can be served with any main dish or by itself accompanied by a stuffed Indian bread. It can be transformed into a very refreshing dip for fried food or into a chat, a hearty salad (see Variations at the end of the recipe).

You may roast the peppers any way you like—on the grill or on a stovetop grill, over a gas flame, or on a rack set on an electric burner, or under the broiler, as in Step 2. You can do this ahead of time. In fact, you can prepare all the vegetables and refrigerate them, separately, for up to one day, then combine them with the yogurt, mint, and salt just before serving.

SERVES 4

> 2 medium green bell peppers
>
> 2 medium red bell peppers
>
> 2 small cucumbers, peeled, seeded, and thinly sliced
>
> 2 cups yogurt
>
> 2 tablespoons minced mint
>
> 2 tablespoons minced red onion
>
> Coarse salt to taste

186

1. Preheat the broiler.

2. Cut the peppers in half and place them, skin side up, under the broiler until charred. Transfer to a paper bag and fold it shut to let the peppers sweat, thus loosening its skin. When the peppers are cool enough to handle, rub the skin off with your fingers. Remove the core and seeds and discard.

3. Cut the peppers into $1/2$-inch pieces and put them in a bowl. Add all the other ingredients and mix until blended. Serve immediately or refrigerate.

Variations:

ROASTED PEPPER DIP:

Working in batches, puree the salad in a food processor or electric blender. Dilute with 1 cup of buttermilk.

CHICKEN AND ROASTED PEPPER CHAT:

Fold $3/4$ pound sliced cooked chicken, $1/2$ cup chopped toasted pecans, 2 teaspoons prepared mustard, and 1 tablespoon mango chutney into the salad.

Carrot and Blackberry Yogurt Salad
with Walnuts

Gajjar Raita

In the valley of Kashmir, this wonderful nutmeg-scented salad is made with freshly picked green walnuts that taste like truffle-scented chestnuts. If you are lucky enough to find them, use them instead of toasted walnuts. You can use toasted pecans, hazelnuts, and macadamia nuts in place of walnuts.

Serves 4

1 cup plain yogurt

2 tablespoons maple syrup or honey

$1/4$ teaspoon grated nutmeg

$1/8$ teaspoon anise seeds, crushed

$1/8$ teaspoon white pepper

$1/2$ pound carrots, peeled and finely diced

2 cups blackberries

1 cup chopped green or toasted walnuts

Whip the yogurt, maple syrup, nutmeg, anise seeds, and white pepper in a bowl until thoroughly blended. Top with the carrots, blackberries, and walnuts. Fold the salad gently and serve.

MINT CHUTNEY

Podina Chatni

This fresh chutney, very fragrant and only slightly hot, is perfect with fried food, roasted and grilled meats, and tandoori meats.

MAKES 1 CUP

$^2/_3$ cup white wine vinegar

2 tablespoons maple syrup or sugar

4 green chiles, stemmed

1 cube (1 inch) fresh ginger, peeled

1 small green bell pepper, cored and chopped

1 cup (lightly packed) mint leaves

1 cup (lightly packed) fresh coriander
(cilantro) leaves and tender stems

189

Put all the ingredients into the workbowl of an electric blender or food processor. Process, turning off and on and pushing the herbs down with a rubber spatula, until reduced to a sauce. Transfer to a small bowl and serve immediately or refrigerate.

Coconut Chutney

Narial Chatni

Imbued with the delicate sweetness of coconut and spices, this uncooked chutney goes well with all fish, seafood, and poultry dishes. What makes this recipe special is that you can use commercially available sweetened coconut flakes. As a result, you can put together the chutney in a matter of seconds. It is fine to purée fresh coriander stems, but not mint, as its stems tend to be fibrous.

Serves 4

> 1 cup yogurt
>
> 1 cup (packed) sweetened coconut flakes
>
> 1 to 2 jalapeños, stemmed and sliced, with seeds
>
> 1 large clove garlic, peeled
>
> 1 piece ($\frac{1}{2}$ inch) fresh ginger, peeled
>
> $\frac{1}{4}$ cup (lightly packed) fresh coriander (cilantro) leaves and tender stems
>
> 4 mint leaves
>
> Coarse salt to taste
>
> 1 teaspoon roasted cumin seeds

Combine the yogurt, coconut, jalapeños, garlic, ginger, coriander, mint, and salt in an electric blender or a food processor and process until finely pureed. Transfer to a bowl. Check the seasoning and add more salt if necessary. Stir in the cumin seeds and serve immediately or refrigerate.

GARLIC-TOMATO CHUTNEY

Lassan Chatni

Try this hot garlic chutney with roast or grilled meat or for a change of pace, spoon it over a pilaf or spread it on an Indian bread. The dried chiles are left in the chutney, but take care—they are too hot to eat.

MAKES 2 CUPS

> 1 1/2 pounds tomatoes, peeled, seeded, and sliced
>
> 2 jalapeños, stemmed and minced with seeds
>
> 1 tablespoon grated fresh ginger
>
> 1/4 cup vegetable oil
>
> 6 dried red chiles
>
> 1 1/2 teaspoons *Panch Phoron* (page 8)
>
> 8 large garlic cloves, peeled and thickly sliced
>
> Coarse salt to taste

1. Combine the tomatoes, jalapeños, and ginger in a bowl.

2. Heat the oil in a heavy pan over medium-high heat. Add the dried chiles and fry until almost black, about 2 minutes. Reduce the heat to medium-low and add the *Panch Phoron* and garlic. Fry the spices until they turn several shades darker and the garlic light brown, about 2 minutes. Add the tomato mixture and cook, uncovered, over low heat for 35 minutes, or until the chutney is thick and pulpy and the oil separates, stirring occasionally. Turn off the heat and stir in the salt. Cool completely before using.

Sweet Mango Chutney

Aam Chatni

Make this classic mango chutney in early spring when unripe green mangoes appear at vegetable markets. It is astonishingly easy to prepare—all you do is combine all the ingredients and cook down the sauce to the consistency of jam. Mango chutney is sweetish hot and goes with any number of dishes. I particularly like it with lamb and chicken preparations.

MAKES 2 CUPS

SYRUP

1 1/2 cups sugar

1/2 cup wine vinegar

1 teaspoon minced garlic

1 tablespoon ground ginger

3 tablespoons dry mustard

1/4 teaspoon ground cloves

1/4 teaspoon ground cinnamon

1/2 teaspoon ground red pepper

3 small firm, unripe mangoes (1 pound), peeled and cut into 1-inch pieces

FRUIT AND NUTS

1/4 cup dark raisins

1/4 cup slivered almonds

192

1. Combine all the ingredients for the syrup in a stainless steel or enameled pan and bring to a boil over low heat, stirring often. Simmer until thick and syrupy, about 15 minutes.

2. Add the mango pieces and continue to cook for 10 minutes, or until the mango looks translucent. Turn off the heat. Add the raisins and almonds and serve warm or spoon into sterilized jars. When completely cool, cover and store. (*The chutney keeps well, for up to 3 weeks in the refrigerator.*)

Peach Chutney
with Walnuts and Saffron

Khoobani Chatni

This peach chutney is a far cry from commercially prepared products. It is a delicious and irresistible example of the play of spices and flavor for which Indian cooking is justifiably famous. Seasoned with ginger, mustard, fennel, pepper, and saffron, it adds power and pizzazz to roasts and grills. It beautifully complements the Parsi Breaded Shrimp in Green Paste (page 124) as well as Tandoori Chicken (page 90).

Makes 4 cups

2 pounds peaches, peeled, pitted, and sliced (4 cups)

1 cup white wine vinegar

1 1/2 cups (packed) light brown sugar

2 tablespoons julienned fresh ginger

1/2 teaspoon saffron threads

1 teaspoon yellow mustard seeds

1 teaspoon fennel seeds

1/2 teaspoon crushed red pepper

1 cup dark raisins

1 cup walnuts

1. Put the peaches in a large stainless steel or enameled pan. Add the vinegar and bring to a boil over medium-high heat. Cook the peaches until barely tender but not cooked through, about 7 minutes. Turn off the heat and let the peaches sit in the liquid for 5 minutes. Using a slotted spoon, transfer the fruit to a bowl, leaving the liquid in the pan.

2. Add the brown sugar, ginger, saffron, mustard, fennel, and red pepper to the liquid in the pan and bring back to a boil over high heat. Boil until the syrup turns sticky, about 12 minutes. Add the reserved peaches and continue to cook until the chutney looks thick and glazed like a jam, about 8 minutes. Turn off the heat and fold in the raisins and walnuts. Spoon the chutney into sterilized jars. Seal or cover and refrigerate. Let the chutney ripen for 1 day before serving.

Variation: _____

NECTARINE CHUTNEY WITH WALNUTS AND SAFFRON:

Substitute fresh nectarines for the peaches.

195

INDIAN SALSA

Kachoomar

The relish kachoomar is used primarily to add moisture to a meal. Not surprisingly it goes well with stuffed breads, tandoori meats, roasts, and grilled chicken, lamb, and beef. Unlike Mexican salsa, which can range in heat from mild to dynamite-hot, Indian Salsa is mild and fragrant. Particularly nice additions to the basic mix of tomatoes, chiles, cucumbers, and onions are daikon radish and Kirby cucumbers.

SERVES 4

1 cup finely diced tomato, drained

1 tablespoon chopped green chiles

1 cup finely diced cucumber, preferably Kirby

1 cup finely diced red onion

1 cup finely diced radish, preferably daikon

$^1/_2$ cup chopped fresh coriander (cilantro) leaves and tender stems

1 tablespoon lemon juice

Put all the ingredients in a bowl, toss well to mix, and serve. (*The salsa can be prepared ahead and refrigerated for up to 1 day. Bring to room temperature before serving.*)

CUMIN-ONION BUTTER

Masala Ghee

Sometimes called baghar, *this very fragrant spice butter is used as a finishing flavor over lentil purées, soups, and Indian breads. It can also be served as a garnishing butter with pilafs and* biriyani.

MAKES 2/3 CUP

> 6 tablespoons *usli ghee* (see page 216)
>   or vegetable oil
>
> 2 teaspoons cumin seeds
>
> 2 cups chopped onion

1. Heat the *usli ghee* in a large frying pan over medium-high heat. Add the cumin seeds. When they turn several shades darker, add the onion and cook, stirring, until golden brown, about 15 minutes.

2. Transfer to a bowl and serve immediately. Or pour into a jar, let cool, cover, and refrigerate. (*The butter keeps well for up to 4 months in the refrigerator. Heat thoroughly before serving.*)

DESSERTS
AND BEVERAGES

INDIAN desserts are generally mellow milk- and fruit-based puddings that are welcome after a spicy meal. They can be made ahead and kept refrigerated for several days, making them ideal for entertaining.

Lassi, a frothy yogurt drink made with fruits, herbs, or flower essences, and fruit shakes, limeades, and lemonades are popular with Indian food because they counter the heat of the spicy food. Among alcoholic drinks served with Indian food, beer and ale are the most popular, and rightly so, since their malty effervescence complements the fragrant aromas and complex flavors of the food. Wine lovers need not despair, however. Any decent dry red, white, or rosé wine will go admirably as long as it is reasonably robust. Fine wines should be reserved for another occasion—their subtleties will be overpowered and lost when served with Indian food. You may of course serve non-alcoholic beer and wine or ice water as most Indians traditionally do.

QUICK SAFFRON PUDDING

Srikhand

A delicate pudding made with yogurt and flavored with saffron, pistachios, and cardamom, this comes from the state of Gujarat in western India. I find the process of draining yogurt time consuming, so I devised a shortcut. Combine yogurt with sour cream and cream cheese, and you can achieve the same flavor and richness. All this in less than a minute!

SERVES 4

> $1/4$ teaspoon saffron threads, crushed
>
> 1 tablespoon hot milk or water
>
> 1 cup yogurt
>
> $1/3$ cup sour cream
>
> 3 ounces plain cream cheese
>
> $2/3$ cup confectioners' sugar
>
> $1/2$ teaspoon ground cardamom
>
> 2 tablespoons chopped unsalted pistachios

1. Put the saffron threads in bowl. Add the hot milk and let soak for 15 minutes.

2. Add the yogurt, sour cream, cream cheese, and sugar and whip until thoroughly blended and light and fluffy. Stir in the cardamom and half the pistachios. Spoon the pudding into small dessert bowls or stemmed glasses. Sprinkle with the remaining pistachios. Refrigerate for at least 2 hours.

3. Serve chilled.

Variation:

Fold in 2 cups cut-up fresh fruit with the pistachios.

INDIAN RICE PUDDING
with Cardamom

Kheer

Rice pudding is one of the most popular desserts in India. There are many different versions but all have one thing in common: no eggs are used in the pudding. Instead, the milk is cooked down with the rice to a thick creamy consistency. This rice pudding, flavored with cardamom and coconut and garnished with raisins and almonds, is from Bengal, which is famous for its milk desserts.

SERVES 4

> 2 cups whole milk
>
> 3 cups light cream
>
> $1/4$ cup basmati rice
>
> $1/4$ cup sugar
>
> $1/2$ teaspoon ground cardamom
>
> 2 tablespoons sweetened coconut flakes
>
> 2 tablespoons golden raisins
>
> 2 tablespoons sliced almonds

1. Combine the milk and light cream in a medium heavy-bottomed saucepan and bring to a boil over very low heat. Add the rice and simmer for 1 hour, or until the rice is cooked and the milk has reduced and thickened. Stir in the sugar, cardamom, and coconut. (*The pudding will keep, covered, for up to 5 days in the refrigerator.*)

2. Serve warm or chilled, garnished with raisins and almonds.

MANGO FOOL

Mangophul

Fool, a dessert of English origins, became the all-time favorite of Anglo-Indians. Here it is made with mango purée, but it can be done with any ripe fruit; it is particularly good with raspberries.

SERVES 4

1 large ripe mango

$1/2$ teaspoon almond extract

1 tablespoon lemon juice

2 tablespoons orange liqueur (optional)

1 cup light cream

$1/4$ cup sugar

2 tablespoons cornstarch dissolved in
   $1/4$ cup water

1 cup heavy cream, whipped

Mint sprigs, for garnish

1. Peel the mango and cut the flesh away from the pit. Purée the flesh in a food processor. Strain to remove any fibrous parts and put in a bowl. Stir in the almond extract, lemon juice, and liqueur, if using. Set aside.

2. Heat the light cream and sugar in a small saucepan over medium heat. When small bubbles form around the edges of the cream, stir in the cornstarch mixture. Cook until the cream thickens and forms a custard, about 2 minutes. Strain the custard to remove any lumps and cool thoroughly.

3. Combine the mango puree and custard. Fold in the whipped cream and spoon into individual dessert glasses and refrigerate for 2 hours. Serve garnished with mint.

Mango Ice Cream

Aam Kulfi

Indian ice-cream is made without eggs. Milk and cream are cooked down, sweetened, and flavored. Fruit pulp—in this case mango—is stirred in before freezing. The result has a texture somewhere between ice-cream and sorbet. Kulfi are traditionally made in special molds, which are 3-inch-high conical aluminum or stainless steel containers with a lid. The frozen kulfi is pried out with a knife; immersing the mold briefly in hot water aids this process.

SERVES 6

4 cups whole milk

$1^1/_4$ cups heavy cream

$^1/_4$ teaspoon grated nutmeg

5 tablespoons maple syrup or sugar

1 cup mango purée, fresh or canned Indian
Alphonso mango purée

1. Combine the milk and cream in a medium heavy-bottomed saucepan and bring to the boil over medium heat. Reduce the heat and simmer, stirring often, until it reduces by half, to about $2^1/_2$ cups, about 20 minutes. Set aside to cool.

2. When cool, stir in the nutmeg, maple syrup, and mango purée. Pour the mixture into 6 *kulfi* molds or small ramekins, distributing it evenly. Cover with plastic wrap and freeze until set, about 6 hours.

3. To serve, remove the ice cream from the molds by running a sharp knife around the edges. If necessary, dip the mold in hot water to loosen it. Slip each *kulfi* onto a dessert plate, cut across into 3 or 4 slices, and serve.

203

SWEET MANGO LASSI

Aam Lassi

I guarantee that even if you think you don't like yogurt you will love this shake. Combined with mangoes and blended until frothy, lassi is always refreshing, not just at mealtime. The bubbly froth subsides when lassi stands awhile, so whip it again in the blender or with a whisk just before serving.

SERVES 4

> 3 cups yogurt
>
> 1 cup mango purée, fresh or canned Indian
>   Alphonso mango purée
>
> $1/2$ cup sugar
>
> 1 tray ice cubes

Put all the ingredients in an electric blender or food processor and blend until the ice is crushed and the liquid is frothy. Serve immediately in tall glasses. (*The drink will keep, covered, for up to 3 days in the refrigerator. Whip again before serving.*)

SAVORY YOGURT DRINK WITH MINT

Matha

A light drink made with diluted yogurt flavored with mint and cumin, this is a fabulous thirst quencher.

SERVES 4

3 cups plain yogurt

1 cup ice water

1 tablespoon chopped mint leaves

$1/4$ teaspoon ground toasted cumin seeds

1 tray ice cubes

Coarse salt to taste

Put all the ingredients in an electric blender or food processor and blend until the ice is crushed and the liquid is frothy. Serve immediately in tall glasses. (*The drink will keep, covered, for up to 3 days in the refrigerator. Whip again just before serving.*)

GINGER LIMEADE

Shikanji

One of India's most popular beverages, limeade is classically made with an especially aromatic lime called the kagzee nimboo, *meaning paper-skinned lime. The American Key lime is the closest substitute. This drink is very delicious and refreshing, particularly when flavored with ginger.*

SERVES 4

$1/4$ cup lime juice

$1 1/2$ teaspoons ginger juice (see Note)

$3/4$ cup sugar

Ice cubes, for serving

Lime zest, for garnish

1. Combine the lime juice, ginger juice, sugar, and 3 cups water in a tall pitcher and stir until the sugar is dissolved. Refrigerate for at least 2 hours.

2. To serve, fill tall glasses with ice cubes, pour the limeade over, and garnish with a twist of lime zest.

NOTE: To extract ginger juice, press peeled and chopped ginger through a garlic press. Two tablespoons ginger will yield $1 1/2$ teaspoons juice.

SPICED TEA

Chai

The famous Indian spiced tea served in all Indian restaurants, chai is very refreshing to sip at any time of day, not just at the end of a spicy Indian meal. Generally, Indians drink their tea like the English, with sugar and milk. For Spiced Tea, it's best to use an Indian raw sugar, jaggery, that tastes like maple sugar rather than refined white sugar. I like this tea without the milk, but I added it as an option for those who want it. With or without the milk, this tea is truly magical.

SERVES 4

> 1 stick (3-inch) cinnamon
>
> 8 green cardamom pods, bruised
>
> 4 whole cloves
>
> 4 heaping teaspoons loose tea or 4 tea bags, preferably orange pekoe or Darjeeling tea
>
> 2 to 3 tablespoons jaggery, to taste, crushed
>
> 4 1/2 cups boiling water
>
> 1/3 cup scalded milk (optional)

1. Place the spices, tea, and jaggery in a warmed 8-cup teapot and pour the boiling water over them. Cover the teapot with a potholder and let the tea and spices steep for 3 minutes.

2. To serve, strain into cups and pass the milk, if desired.

THE INDIAN PANTRY

Here is a checklist of spices, herbs, and other flavorings frequently called for in Indian cooking. Detailed descriptions follow.

SPICES, HERBS, AND SEASONINGS

Ajowan
Anise seeds
Asafetida
Bay leaves
Cardamom, green pods and seeds
Chiles, green
Cinnamon, sticks and ground
Cloves, whole and ground
Coriander seeds, whole and ground
Coriander leaves (cilantro)
Cumin seeds, whole and ground, toasted
Curry Powder (page 6)
Fennel seeds
Fenugreek seeds
Garam Masala (page 7)
Ginger, fresh and ground
Kari leaves, fresh or dried
Mint
Mustard, seeds and powder
Nigella seeds
Nutmeg
Panch Phoron (page 8)
Paprika
Peppercorns, black, white, green
Pepper, crushed, red
Pepper, ground red

Saffron, threads
Salt, coarse
Tamarind, paste or powder
Turmeric

COCONUT

Coconut flakes sweetened and unsweetened
Coconut milk, fresh or canned
Coconut powder

JAGGERY

OILS, FLAVORINGS, AND OTHERS

Mustard oil
Spice-infused oils
Usli ghee

GRAINS AND LENTILS

Basmati rice
Chapati flour
Chick-pea flour
Lentils, red
Yellow split peas

NUTS

Almonds, Pistachios, and Cashew

RAISINS

Dark and Golden

LENTIL WAFERS

GLOSSARY

An Indian kitchen is usually stocked with spices and dried herbs; lentils, peas, and beans; nuts and seeds; and oils and essences. Following are descriptions of the more common ingredients of Indian cooking.

AJOWAN. (*AJWAIN*) Also known as carum, these tiny seeds resemble celery seeds. When slightly crushed, they give off an aroma similar to thyme. Ajowan is used with vegetables, fish, and shellfish, breads and crackers, and especially beans and peas, since it counters flatulence. Thyme makes a good flavor substitute.

ANISE SEEDS (*SAUNF*) The tiny oval seeds of anise release the same aroma as fennel when crushed, though milder. Indian cooks prefer its subtle flavor to that of fennel. Anise and fennel are interchangeable in recipes.

ASAFETIDA (*HEENG*) This is a strong-smelling spice, available in powdered form. It is used by certain religious groups in India to give a garliclike flavor to food since they are forbidden to use garlic as a seasoning. Not surprisingly, a little chopped garlic can be substituted for asafetida.

BASMATI RICE Basmati means queen of fragrance in Hindi, and that is what this distinctive long-grain rice from India is. Naturally scented with buttery-almond flavor, the grains do not turn mushy or sticky when cooked. Basmati rice is widely available in health food stores and many supermarkets.

BAY (*TEJ PATTA*) Indian bay, the spicy and aromatic leaf of the cassia tree, is an essential spice in North Indian cooking. It is used in Moghul pilafs and curries and in the indispensible spice blend *Garam Masala*. Indian bay is available in Indian grocery stores. Commonly available bay leaf, which comes from the laurel tree, makes an acceptable substitute.

CARDAMOM (*ELAICHI*) These are small, long green or white pods containing highly aromatic tiny black seeds. Cardamom is used either in the pod, as in pilafs and curries, or ground, in desserts and sauces. If used whole, the pods are discarded before serving. For ground cardamom, the pods are hulled, and the seeds separated from the membrane and ground to a powder.

CHAPATI FLOUR (*ATTA*) Chapati flour is finely ground whole wheat kernels with the germ and husk intact. It is rich in nutrients and flavor. Dough made with this flour is easy to roll. Stone-ground whole wheat flour can be substituted.

CHICK-PEA FLOUR (*BESAN*) Dried chick peas are ground into a fine flour. Chick-pea flour is used in batters to give a rich flavor and crackling texture.

CINNAMON (*DALCHINI*) In Indian cooking, cinnamon is used in stick form to lend a subtle fragrance to pilaf and meat dishes and to add spice to tea infusions.

CLOVE (*LAUNG*) Fragrant and pungent, cloves are used both whole and ground in Indian cooking. Whole cloves are used when it is important not to tint the color of the dish, as in white rice pilaf and certain fish preparations. Remove the cloves before serving.

COCONUT (*NARIAL*) Coconut is extensively used in Indian cooking. Grated coconut is used to add texture and visual interest, coconut milk to give a sweet, rich flavor to a sauce. Excellent quality processed coconut is available in grated, milk, cream, and powder forms in Asian grocery stores. Light or heavy cream can be substituted for coconut milk to approximate the texture, with 2 tablespoons of coconut flakes for each cup of cream added, to approximate the flavor. Unsweetened coconut flakes can be substituted for freshly grated coconut. Freshly grated coconut and fresh coconut milk are simple to make.

> *GRATED COCONUT* Buy a medium-size coconut that has no cracks and is heavy with liquid. Pierce the eyes of the coconut with a chisel, drain off the liquid, and discard. Place the coconut in a preheated 375° oven for 25 minutes. Remove the coconut and hit it with a hammer to crack it open and release the meat inside. Peel off the brown skin and cut the meat/flesh into 1-inch pieces. Working in batches, grind the coconut in a food processor. One medium coconut will yield about 2 cups grated coconut. Grated coconut keeps for 5 days in the refrigerator, and 6 months in the freezer, stored in tightly sealed containers.

> *COCONUT MILK* Add 1¼ cups boiling water or milk to 1 cup grated coconut and let soak for 15 minutes. Working in batches, puree the mixture in a blender or food processor. Strain through a double layer of cheesecloth, squeezing the pulp to extract as much liquid as possible. One medium coconut will yield about 2½ cups coconut milk.

CORIANDER SEEDS (*DHANIA SOOKHA*) Yellowish brown and about the size of peppercorns, coriander seeds have a mild and floral aroma. They are used in countless dishes in India, usually ground. Coriander is used in large quantities in both Curry Powder (page 6) and *Garam Masala* (page 7).

CORIANDER LEAVES (*HARA DHANIA*) Fresh coriander, popularly known as cilantro or Chinese parsley, has a pungent aroma quite unlike the seeds of the plant. It is widely used in Indian cooking. Parsley can be substituted for visual appeal, but it lacks the distinctive taste of fresh coriander.

CUMIN SEEDS (*JEERA*) These tiny greenish brown seeds, resembling caraway in shape, are perhaps the most important spice in Indian cooking. Cumin is used both whole and ground and both raw and in toasted form. It is an important component of *Garam Masala* (page 7).

> TOASTED CUMIN SEEDS *Put ¹/₂ cup cumin seeds in a small dry frying pan over medium-high heat. Toast, stirring and shaking, until the seeds are several shades darker and give off their characteristic aroma, about 5 minutes. Transfer to a bowl and let cool. Using a spice mill or a coffee grinder reserved for grinding spices, or a mortar and pestle, grind to a fine powder. (Ground toasted cumin may be stored in an airtight container in a cool, dry place for 3 weeks.)*

CURRY POWDER This spice blend from southern India works magic when creatively employed. In Indian cooking it is used in soups, stews, and sauces and vegetable dishes. Curry Powder is widely available, but it is also very easy to make at home (see page 6).

FENNEL (*SAUNF*) Fennel seeds, tiny and pale green in color, look like cumin or caraway seeds. Ground, they are used in sauces, sweets, and desserts. In Bengal, whole fennel seeds are cooked with vegetables and lentils. Fennel is an excellent digestive and a mouth refresher; it is frequently chewed by Indians like an after-dinner mint. Anise seeds can be substituted.

FENUGREEK (*METHI*) These tiny, brown, bitter-tasting beans are an important spice, particularly in southern and eastern India. Known to counter flatulence, fenugreek is often added to starchy vegetables and legumes. Dill seeds can be substituted.

FLOWER ESSENCES (*RUH*) In Indian cooking, flower essences, such as rose (*gulab*) and Asian pine (*kewra*), are used to provide fragrance in much the same way as vanilla or almond extract. Flower essences are available in Indian and Middle Eastern grocery stores.

GARAM MASALA This highly aromatic blend of spices was created to season the Moghul dishes of northern India. It is sprinkled on or folded into a finished dish to give it a roasted flavor. *Garam Masala* is is commercially available, but it can also be made easily at home (see page 7).

GINGER, FRESH (*ADRAK*) Fresh ginger, the aromatic rhizome used extensively in Asian cooking, is important also in Indian cooking. It is used with vegetables and legumes, in pilafs and stews, in chutneys, and in herbal tea infusions. Since ginger is regarded as a digestive, it is added to dried beans and peas and starchy vegetables. Fresh ginger is always peeled, using a peeler or paring knife, and then grated, crushed, chopped, or sliced. (*Fresh ginger keeps, loosely covered, for several weeks in a refrigerator.*) If fresh ginger is unavailable, ground ginger may be substituted (1 teaspoon ground ginger for 1 tablespoon fresh ginger).

GINGER, GROUND (*SONTH*) Ground ginger is made by powdering sun-dried slices of fresh ginger. It is used in Kashmiri meat dishes, kebabs, relishes, chutneys, sweets, desserts, and beverages. Although ground ginger can be substituted for fresh ginger, the two really aren't similar in taste. Ground ginger is sweet and woody while fresh ginger is spicy and herbal. Try to use the type specified in the recipe.

CHILE, GREEN (*HARA MIRCH*) Green chiles add a herbal aroma as well as heat to a dish. If green chiles are unavailable, substitute 1/4 teaspoon ground red pepper for 1 green chile. For a milder taste seed the chiles. For more of a herbal flavor, add a little chopped green bell pepper with the chiles. Chiles should be handled with care as they cause a burning sensation and irritation when touched. You may want to use rubber or surgical gloves to protect your hands. Take care not to rub your eyes. Be sure to wash your hands with soapy water after handling chiles.

JAGGERY (*GUDH*) Jaggery is unrefined cane or palm sugar. It is used in Indian cooking to lend a sweet taste and a maple-like flavor to the dish. Maple syrup or maple sugar can be substituted.

KARI LEAF (*KARI PATTA*) Kari leaf is an herb, not a spice. It should not be confused with Curry Powder, a blend of several spices (see page 6). Kari leaves have a most captivating aroma, reminiscent of juniper berries and lime. They are used to flavor all types of savory preparations. Kari is better used fresh, though dried is acceptable. Fresh and dried kari leaves are available in Indian grocery stores.

213

LENTILS, RED (*MASAR DAL*) Red lentils, also called pink, are the most popular in Indian cooking because they cook quickly (in about 15 minutes) and are very easy to digest. They are cooked into thick purees, seasoned with spices, and served accompanied with rice or bread. Red lentils are widely available at health food stores.

LENTIL WAFERS (*PUPPADUM OR PAPAD*) These dried, paper-thin rounds are made from lentil or bean flour in a variety of flavors, ranging from plain to black pepper and garlic to green chile and cumin. When you fry them, they puff up (see page 23). They are available at Indian grocery stores.

MINT (*PODINA*) Mint was the favorite herb of the Moghuls, who used it in their pilafs, kebabs, and special lamb dishes. Spearmint is preferred to peppermint. Use fresh mint rather than dried. If necessary, substitute, 1 teaspoon dried mint for 1 tablespoon chopped fresh mint.

MUSTARD OIL (*SARSOON KA TEL*) Mustard seeds are pressed to yield a very aromatic, amber colored oil that is widely used in the cooking of northern and eastern India. Because of its high smoking point, mustard oil is used for deep-frying. It is also used to flavor fish, shellfish, vegetables, and legumes. Mustard oil is available in Indian grocery and specialty stores.

MUSTARD SEEDS (*SARSOON*) These tiny round seeds, brown, black, red, or yellow, look like large poppy seeds. They are added to hot oil (always put the lid on since they spatter) and fried until they pop and release their fragrance. This mustard-infused oil is a prized seasoning in southern and eastern India. There is very little difference in flavor between various types of mustard seeds, so use whichever is available. Dry mustard and prepared mustard are also used in Indian cooking.

NIGELLA (*KALONJI*) These tiny, black teardrop-shaped seeds have a satiny sheen and a distinct celerylike taste. They have a natural affinity for fish, shellfish, and starchy vegetables. Because they are so beautiful, nigella seeds are always used whole. Also called black onion seeds.

NUTMEG (*JAIPHUL*) The Moghuls had a fondness for this spice and used it quite liberally in their pilafs and braised meats. Nutmeg is also used in sweets, desserts, and chutneys. Buy whole nutmeg and grate it as needed.

PANCH PHORON A classic from eastern India, this is a simple blend of five whole spices: cumin, fennel, mustard seeds, fenugreek, and nigella. It is used to make a spice-infused oil for cooking seafood, vegetables, and legumes. Preblended *Panch*

Phoron is available in Indian grocery stores, but it can be made easily at home (see page 8).

PANEER Soft, moist, and crumbly and imbued with lemon scent, the freshly made Indian cheese *paneer* is nourishing and flavorful. In Indian cooking *paneer* is used crumbled and in cubes. It is available at Indian grocery stores. Farmers cheese and tofu can be substituted. Making *paneer* is very simple.

> PANEER: *Bring 2 quarts milk to a boil. Add 3 1/2 tablespoons lemon juice and continue to cook, stirring, until the milk curdles and separates into curds and whey. Strain the curds through a colander lined with a double layer of cheese-cloth. When cool enough to handle, gather together the corners of the cheesecloth and squeeze gently to extract as much liquid as possible. Remove the cheese from the cheesecloth, wrap tightly in plastic, and refrigerate. (The cheese will keep for 5 days in the refrigerator.) Makes 1 cup.*

PAPRIKA (*DEGHI MIRCH*) Paprika is dried and ground red pepper. Indian paprika, called *deghi mirch*, is different from the Hungarian, Spanish, or California paprika that we are more familiar with. Indian paprika, produced in Kashmir and Goa has a pungent aroma like cayenne, but with the spice's characteristic sweet flavor. Other paprika may be substituted. All paprika should be stored in the refrigerator.

PEPPER, BLACK (*GOL MIRCH*) Black pepper has been in India since ancient times. It is used extensively in all regions of India and in all kinds of dishes, including beverages and baking. While all peppercorns deliver the characteristic bite and scent, Tellicherry peppercorns are the most pungent and aromatic. Buy whole peppercorns and grind them as needed.

PEPPER, WHITE (*SAFAID MIRCH*) White and black pepper are essentially the same except that white peppercorns are hulled to expose the grayish-white berries, unlike black peppercorns, which still have the dark skin attached. Because of their light color and delicate flavor, white peppercorns are preferred in cream sauces and soups, fruit salads, and certain fish and shellfish preparations of Anglo-Indian origin.

PEPPER, GROUND RED (*LAL MIRCH*) This is the red devil's powder that gives food a hot taste. By adding more or less of it, you can regulate the heat of a dish. Dried red chile pods ground to a powder, crushed red pepper, or fresh green chiles can be substituted.

SAFFRON (*KESAR OR ZAFFRAN*) Saffron is the most expensive spice in the world. The Moghuls loved and used it to flavor and color pilafs and meat casseroles. Saffron is also used in desserts, sweets, chutneys, and beverages. Buy only saffron threads, the pure form of the spice.

SALT (*NAWAK*) Salt is an essential component of Indian cooking not only to enhance but also to extract the flavor of spices and herbs. For general cooking, I prefer sea salt for its texture and purity.

SILVER LEAF (*VARK*) An edible paper-thin tissue of pure silver used as an adornment on foods for special occasions. If silver leaf is unavailable, omit it from the recipe. None of the recipes in this book call for *vark*.

SPICE-INFUSED OIL (*TADKA*) *Tadka* means exploded and that is exactly what happens when whole spices are added to very hot oil. In the *tadka* process, oil is heated in a small pan until very hot. Whole spices are then added and fried until they release their fragrance into the oil. This spice-infused oil is used as a base for dressing salads and for cooking vegetables, pilafs, chutneys, and other preparations. The three most popular *tadkas* of Indian cooking are: cumin *tadka* from North India, mustard *tadka* from South India, and *Panch Phoron tadka* from eastern India.

TAMARIND (*IMLI*) Tamarind pulp, brownish-black in color with a distinctive sour taste, is used to flavor various soups, stews, sauces, chutneys, and relishes. Tamarind chutney and tamarind tea infusions are very popular in India. Tamarind is sold in 1-pound blocks, as a paste, and as powder. Pitted prunes combined with a little lemon juice or pomegranate molasses may be substituted.

TURMERIC (*HALDI*) This spice colors everything it touches yellow. It is one of the main ingredients of Curry Powder. Used in moderation, turmeric imparts a woody scent and light lemon color to pilafs, vegetables, and legumes.

USLI GHEE This melted and browned butter has a characteristic caramel-fudge aroma. It is used for pouring over *dal*, where a mere half teaspoon lends a mountain of flavor, for finishing fish or meat, and for cooking, mainly pilafs, legumes, breads, desserts, sweets, and some soups. For centuries the more common cooking medium has been, and still is, oils, such as sesame, peanut, mustard, and coconut oils. Clarified butter or vegetable oil can be substituted for *usli ghee*.

> USLI GHEE: *Melt and simmer 1/2 pound (2 sticks) unsalted butter in a pan over low heat until it stops crackling and the residue at the bottom turns golden brown, about 25 minutes. When cool, strain off the clear liquid into a jar. Refrigerate or freeze. Makes 3/4 cup.*

YELLOW SPLIT PEAS (*CHANNA DAL*) Indian yellow split peas are the staple legume eaten by 700 million vegetarians in India. High in nutrients, they have many uses in Indian cooking, from soups and stews to dumplings, breads, and pancakes. The yellow split peas sold in American supermarkets are an acceptable substitute, but they are different botanically. Indian yellow split peas are meatier tasting and less gummy when cooked than their American counterpart.

YOGURT (*DAHI*) Yogurt is used in India to make sauces velvety and to mellow curries, and it is consumed as a salad, a dessert, and a beverage. To prevent the yogurt from separating when adding it to a warm sauce, lightly whip the yogurt first to stabilize it. Non-fat yogurt is fine in Indian cooking, but low-fat and whole milk yogurt will give creamier results. The choice is yours.

217

Mail Order Services

Adriana's Caravan
409 Vanderbilt Street
Brooklyn, NY 11218
(800) 316-0820

Bombay Emporium
294 Craft Avenue
Pittsburgh, PA 15213
(412) 648-4965

Bazaar of India
1810 University Avenue
Berkeley, CA 947002
(510) 548-4110

Foods of India, Sinha Trading Company
121 Lexington Avenue
New York, NY 10016
(212) 683-4419

India Gifts and Food
1031 West Belmont Avenue
Chicago, IL 60657
(773) 348-4392

India Spices and Grocery
5891 West Pico Avenue
Los Angeles, CA 90010
(213) 931-4871

Indian Grocery Store
2342 Douglas Road
Coral Gables, FL 33134
(305) 448-5869

Penzey's Spice House, Ltd.
P.O. Box 1448
Waukesha, WI 53187
(414) 574-0278

Julie Sahni's Savory Spices & Herbs, Ltd.
P.O. Box 023792
Brooklyn, NY 11202
(718) 625-4865

The Souk
1916 Pike Place North
Seattle, WA 98101
(206) 441-1666

TABLE OF EQUIVALENTS

The ingredients in this book are measured in the standard American cup (8 ounces), tablespoon (16 tablespoons to a cup), and teaspoon (3 teaspoons to a tablespoon). For your convenience weight equivalents for the most commonly used staples are provided in both ounces and grams and liquid equivalents in both ounces and milliliters.

WEIGHT EQUIVALENTS

	CHAPATI FLOUR		BASMATI RICE		LENTILS		JAGGERY		RAISINS		ALMONDS	
	oz	g	oz	g	oz	g	oz	g	oz	g	oz	g
1/4 CUP	1	30	1 1/2	45	1 1/2	45	1 1/2	45	1	30	1	30
1/3 CUP	1 1/2	45	2	60	2	60	2	60	2	60	2	60
1/2 CUP	2	60	2 1/2	75	3	90	3	90	3	90	2 1/2	75
1 CUP	4	120	5	150	6	180	6	180	6	180	5	150

LIQUID EQUIVALENTS (for milk, cream, yogurt, coconut milk, and stock, etc.)

	U.S.	U.K.
	FLUID OUNCES (OZ)	METRIC MILLILITERS (ML)
1/8 CUP	1	30
1/4 CUP	2	60
1/3 CUP	2 1/2	80
1/2 CUP	4	125
1 CUP	8	250

INDEX